1 & 2 TIMOTHY TITUS AND PHILEMON

D0061689

J. Vernon McGee

THOMAS NELSON PUBLISHERS

Nashville • Atlanta • London • Vancouver

Published in Nashville, Tennessee, by Thomas Nelson, Inc.

Scripture quotations are from the KING JAMES VERSION of the Bible.

Library of Congress Cataloging-in-Publication Data

McGee, J. Vernon (John Vernon), 1904–1988
    [Thru the Bible with J. Vernon McGee]
    Thru the Bible commentary series / J. Vernon McGee.
        p.   cm.
    Reprint. Originally published: Thru the Bible with J. Vernon
McGee. 1975.
    Includes bibliographical references.   ·
    ISBN 0-7852-1054-7 (TR)
    ISBN 0-7852-1113-6 (NRM)
    1. Bible—Commentaries. I. Title.
BS491.2.M37   1991
220.7′7—dc20   90–41340
                                                       CIP

PRINTED IN MEXICO
19 20 21 22 23 - 06 05 04

TITUS

PHILEMON

CONTENTS

1 TIMOTHY

2 TIMOTHY

PREFACE

The radio broadcasts of the Thru the Bible Radio five-year program were transcribed, edited, and published first in single-volume paperbacks to accommodate the radio audience.

There has been a minimal amount of further editing for this publication. Therefore, these messages are not the word-for-word recording of the taped messages which went out over the air. The changes were necessary to accommodate a reading audience rather than a listening audience.

These are popular messages, prepared originally for a radio audience. They should not be considered a commentary on the entire Bible in any sense of that term. These messages are devoid of any attempt to present a theological or technical commentary on the Bible. Behind these messages is a great deal of research and study in order to interpret the Bible from a popular rather than from a scholarly (and too-often boring) viewpoint.

We have definitely and deliberately attempted "to put the cookies on the bottom shelf so that the kiddies could get them."

The fact that these messages have been translated into many languages for radio broadcasting and have been received with enthusiasm reveals the need for a simple teaching of the whole Bible for the masses of the world.

I am indebted to many people and to many sources for bringing this volume into existence. I should express my especial thanks to my secretary, Gertrude Cutler, who supervised the editorial work; to Dr. Elliott R. Cole, my associate, who handled all the detailed work with the publishers; and finally, to my wife Ruth for tenaciously encouraging me from the beginning to put my notes and messages into printed form.

Solomon wrote, ". . . of making many books there is no end; and much study is a weariness of the flesh" (Eccl. 12:12). On a sea of books that flood the marketplace, we launch this series of THRU THE BIBLE with the hope that it might draw many to the one Book, *The Bible.*

J. VERNON MCGEE

1 TIMOTHY

The First Epistle to
TIMOTHY

INTRODUCTION

The First Epistle to Timothy introduces us to a new set of epistles which were written by Paul. There are three of them that belong together (1 and 2 Timothy and Titus), and they are called "The Pastoral Epistles," because they have to do with local churches. You will find that these pastoral epistles are in contrast, for instance, to the Epistle to the Ephesians. There Paul speaks of the church as the body of believers who are in Christ and the glorious, wonderful position that the church has. The church which is invisible, made up of *all* believers who are in the body of Christ, *manifests* itself down here upon the earth in local assemblies, in the local churches.

Now, just to put a steeple on a building and a bell in the steeple and a pulpit down front and a choir in the loft singing the doxology doesn't mean it is a local church in the New Testament sense of the word. There must be certain identifying features. I have written a booklet called *The Spiritual Fingerprints of the Visible Church,* in which I point out that a local church must manifest itself in a certain way in order to meet the requirements of a church of the Lord Jesus.

These three epistles were written to two young preachers who worked with Paul: Timothy and Titus. They were a part of his fruit; that is, they were led to Christ through the ministry of Paul. He had these men with him as helpers, and he instructed them about the local church.

In all three epistles Paul is dealing with two things: the *creed* of the church and the *conduct* of the church. For the church within, the worship must be right. For the church outside, good works must be manifested. Worship is inside; works are outside. That's the way the church is to manifest itself.

Paul deals with these two topics in each of the three epistles. For instance, in 1 Timothy, chapter 1, is faith, the *faith* of the church—its doctrine. In chapter 2 is the *order* of the church. Chapter 3 concerns the *officers* of the church. Chapter 4 describes the *apostasy* that was coming, and chapters 5 and 6 tell of the *duties* of the officers.

In 2 Timothy, Paul deals with the *afflictions* of the church in chapter 1 and the *activity* of the church in chapter 2. Then the *apostasy* of the church and the *allegiance* of the church follow in chapters 3 and 4.

Titus has the same theme. Chapter 1 tells of the *order* of the church, chapter 2 is about the *doctrine* of the church, and in chapter 3 is the *good works* of the church.

So there is *creed* on the inside of the church and *conduct* on the outside. Within is worship and without are good works.

The church today manifests itself in a local assembly. It first puts up a building. In Paul's day, they didn't have a building. That's one thing they didn't need because they were not building churches. They generally met in homes and probably in public buildings. We know in Ephesus that Paul used—probably rented—the school of Tyrannus. I suppose Paul used the auditorium during the siesta time each day. People came in from everywhere to hear him preach. That could be characterized as a local assembly, and it became a local church in Ephesus.

In order to be a local assembly, the church must have certain things to characterize it. It must have a creed, and its doctrine must be accurate. There are two verses that summarize Paul's message in these epistles: "As I besought thee to abide still at Ephesus, when I went to Macedonia, that thou mightest charge some that they teach no other [different] doctrine" (1 Tim. 1:3). It is important that a church have *correct* doctrine. That's what I mean when I say that a steeple on a building doesn't make it a local church by any means. Then again Paul said to this young preacher: "But if I tarry long, that thou mayest know how thou oughtest to behave thyself in the house of God, which is the church of the living God, the pillar and ground of the truth" (1 Tim. 3:15). The local church is made up of believers who are members of the body of Christ. In order for them to function, they need leadership. Somebody has to be appointed to sweep the place out and sombody to build a fire in the stove—if they have one.

In the first little church that I served, I swept the church out sometimes, and on Sunday morning, because it was a little country church, the first one who got there built a fire in the stove. I always tried to be a little late, but I'd say that half the time I built the fire. Those things are essential. Also it's nice to have a choir and a song leader. In addition to this, Paul is going to say that officers are essential for a church to be orderly. There must be officers, and they must meet certain requirements. The church should function in an orderly manner and manifest itself in the community by its good works. Unfortunately today that is idealistic in most places because the local church doesn't always manifest what it should.

From these Pastoral Epistles have come three different types of church government which have been used by the great denominations of the church. The churches never disagreed on doctrine in the old days as much as they disagreed on this matter of church government, that is, how the local church is to function. I marvel that they could get three different forms of government out of these three Pastoral Epistles, but they did.

1. There is the *episcopal* form of government where there is one man, or maybe several men, who are in charge at the top. The Roman Catholic church calls that man a pope. In other churches he is called the archbishop; if there are several leaders, they are called bishops. The Church of England and other churches follow the episcopal form of government. They are controlled by men at the top who are outside the local church.

2. Another form of church government is known as the *presbyterian* or representative form of government. The local church elects certain men from its membership, called elders and deacons, to be officers, and the government of the local church is in their hands. Unfortunately, the churches were bound together by an organization above the level of the local church, and that organization could control the local church.

3. The third type of church government is the opposite extreme

from the episcopal form, called the *congregational* form of government. You see it, of course, in the Congregational and Baptist churches. The *people* are the ones who make the decisions and who are actually in control. The entire church votes on taking in members and on everything else that concerns the local church.

Perhaps you are wondering how they could get three forms of church government from the same words in the Pastoral Epistles. Well, of course, certain words were interpreted differently. I'll try to call attention to these various interpretations as we go through the Pastoral Epistles.

The very interesting thing is that in the early days all three forms of church government functioned and seemed to work well. But in recent years all three forms of government have fallen on evil days; they don't seem to work as they once did. Men who are members of all three forms of government tell me that there is internal strife and disorder and dissension. What is wrong? Immediately somebody says, "Well, the *system* is wrong."

This is an interesting question since we have a representative form of civil government in this country. It was patterned after the church government. You see, the early colonists didn't want a king. That was the only form of government they had known, and they had had enough of a king. They did not want an autocratic form of government, and they were rather reluctant to let the people rule. That may seem strange to you when you listen to local politicians today who talk about "everybody having a vote." In colonial times women didn't vote; men who were not landowners did not vote. Only those who had property and belonged to a certain elite class voted.

The reason the colonists did not want a king to rule over them was because they couldn't trust human nature, which means they couldn't trust each other. We think of those men as being wonderful, political patriotic saints. Well, they were human beings and filled with foibles. They knew they couldn't trust each other, so they would not put power in the hands of one man. They were also afraid to put power in the people's hands because they had no confidence in the people either.

That contradicts the concept that the politician purports when he says that the majority can't be wrong—or "The voice of the people is the voice of God." Frankly, that's just not true.

Why is it, then, that our forms of church government are not working as they should? Well, I want to say—and I hope I'm not misunderstood, because I recognize my inability to express it in the way I'd like to express it to you—that I believe Paul is saying in this epistle that the form of government, important as it is, is not as important as the caliber and character of the men who are holding office.

These epistles outline certain requirements for officers, such as being sober, having one wife, etc. These requirements are essential and are the subjects of debate in the local churches. But here is something more important that I have never heard argued in my forty long years as a pastor, and that is the most *basic* requirement for officers. Paul is trying to convey to us that the men who are officers must be *spiritual,* because no system will function unless the men who are in the place and position of authority are right. If they are wrong, no system—whether it is congregational or episcopal or presbyterian—will *work.*

That, my friend, is the problem. It is the problem today in politics, and it is the problem today in the church. When we elect a man, he must be successful in his vocation and he should have leadership ability. I think those are good requirements, but we need to determine if he is a *spiritual* man.

Paul is going to emphasize two aspects of the spiritual officer: he must be a man of *faith,* and he must be motivated by *love.* Unless those two characteristics are operating in his life, the officer can't function in the church no matter how much ability he has.

What this simply means is that the authority the officers have is actually no authority at all. Paul says that when you've been made an elder or a bishop or a deacon in the church, you have an office and you may feel very pompous and authoritative, but Paul says you really have no authority. Well, what does he mean? He means that *Christ* is the Head of the church, and the *Holy Spirit* is the One to give the leading and the guiding and the direction. The officer is never to assert *his* will in anything; he is to find out what the will of God is. That means he will have to be a man of faith.

He also will have to be motivated by love. Now that doesn't mean that he is to go around soft-soaping everybody and scratching their backs, trying to be a man-pleaser, but he is to carry through the *will of Christ* in that church. It is his job to make sure that Christ is the Head of the church. Oh, how I've spent weary hours in board meetings talking about some little thing that had absolutely nothing to do with the spiritual welfare of the church, but had a lot to do with the will of some hardheaded, stubborn officer who thought he was a spiritual man. Such a man had no idea that he was to carry through the will of Christ because, to begin with, he had never sought the will of Christ. All he was attempting to do was to serve his own will because he thought his will was right.

Oh, my friend, Christ is the Head of the local church today. We see this is the very first verse where Paul calls Him "the Lord Jesus Christ." He is the *Lord*, and, remember, that means He is Number One. The Lord Jesus said in His day, "And why call ye me, Lord, Lord, and do not the things which I say?" (Luke 6:46). A lot of people call Him "Lord" today in the church, and they're not following Him at all. To be an officer in the church means that you're to carry through the will of Christ, His commandments, and His desires. He is the Head of the local church. That is what is needed today, is it not?

Therefore, I am not prepared to argue with anybody about the form of government in his church. If you think yours is the best form, fine! You go along with it. But it will work only if you have the right men. It won't work—no matter what the form is—if you have the wrong men. The unspiritual officer is the monkey wrench in the machinery of the church today. Although it is the business of the church to get Him through to the world, that is the reason we don't see much evidence of Christ.

In 1 Timothy, then, we deal with the nitty-gritty of the local church, with the emphasis that it is the character and caliber of her leaders that will determine whether the church is really a church of the Lord Jesus Christ.

OUTLINE

I. The Faith of the Church, Chapter 1
A. Introduction, Chapter 1:1-2
B. Warning against Unsound Doctrine, Chapter 1:3-10
C. Personal Testimony of Paul, Chapter 1:11-17
D. Charge to Timothy, Chapter 1:18-20

II. Public Prayer and Woman's Place in the Churches, Chapter 2
A. Public Prayer for the Public and Public Officials, Chapter 2:1-7
B. How Men Are to Pray, Chapter 2:8
C. How Women Are to Pray, Chapter 2:9-15

III. Officers in the Churches, Chapter 3
A. Requirements for Elders, Chapter 3:1-7
B. Requirements for Deacons, Chapter 3:8-13
C. Report of Paul to Timothy, Chapter 3:14-16

IV. Apostasy in the Churches, Chapter 4
A. How to Recognize the Apostles, Chapter 4:1-5
B. What the "Good Minister" Can Do in Times of Apostasy, Chapter 4:6-16

V. Duties of Officers of the Churches, Chapters 5 and 6
A. Relationship of Ministers to Different Groups in the Local Church, Chapter 5
B. Relationship of Believers to Others, Chapter 6

CHAPTER 1

THEME: The faith of the church

Paul's emphasis here will not be a doctrinal statement of the Christian church, but a warning against false teachers in the local church. He will stress that the gospel of the grace of God is central in doctrine and concerns the person of Christ.

INTRODUCTION

The introduction to 1 Timothy is unlike any other in Paul's epistles. Perhaps you had come to the conclusion that they were all the same, but the introductions to the Pastoral Epistles are a little different. Dr. Marvin R. Vincent has said that the salutation in 1 Timothy as a whole has no parallel in Paul.

> **Paul, an apostle of Jesus Christ by the commandment of God our Saviour, and Lord Jesus Christ, which is our hope;**
>
> **Unto Timothy, my own son in the faith: Grace, mercy, and peace, from God our Father and Jesus Christ our Lord [1 Tim. 1:1–2].**

"Paul, an apostle of Jesus Christ by the commandment of God." Paul asserts his apostleship to Timothy, and he has certainly done so before. In Ephesians he says, "Paul, an apostle of Jesus Christ by the *will* of God . . ." (Eph. 1:1, italics mine). Now what is the difference between the *commandment* and the *will* of God? The will of God and the commandment of God are the same, yet they are not exactly synonymous. All the commandments which you will find in the Bible reveal the will of God. This would include much more than the Ten Commandments. For example, we are told that it is the will of God that we pray: "Pray without ceasing. In every thing give thanks: for this is the will of God in Christ Jesus concerning you" (1 Thess. 5:17–18). There are many things which are the will of God, and they are expressed in His commandments. However, I do not think that we have revealed to us all of the will of God, even in the sum total of the commandments in Scripture. The will of God is therefore a much broader term than the commandment of God.

Remember, however, that we have revealed to us enough of the will of God to know that man is *not* saved by obedience to the commandments of God. This is important to reiterate as there are so many today who say the Law is essential to our salvation.

In verse 8 of this chapter, Paul writes, "But we know that the law is good, if a man use it lawfully." How are we to use the Law? First, we need to see that the Law *is* good: "Wherefore the law is holy, and the commandment holy, and just, and good" (Rom. 7:12). It is the very fact that the Law is good and demands absolute goodness from man (in whom there is no good thing) that the sinner cannot obey it. Paul says, "For I know that in me (that is, in my flesh,) dwelleth no good thing . . ." (Rom. 7:18). The Law or the commandments of God were given to *reveal the will of God* and to show that in order for a sinner to be saved it is necessary to find a way other than obedience to a perfect law; to understand this is to use the law "lawfully."

The glory of the gospel is that God found a way that He might be just *and* the justifier of him that believeth in Jesus. In Acts Paul preached: "Be it known unto you therefore, men and brethren, that through this man [that is, the Lord Jesus] is preached unto you the forgiveness of sins: And by him all that believe are justified from all things, from which ye could not be justified by the law of Moses" (Acts 13:38–39). Why could they not be justified by the law of Moses? Because it was a ministration of death: the Law condemned them. The Law wasn't given to save us, but to reveal that God is holy and that you and I are not holy. The way that God found to save us is the way of the Cross, the way of the Lord Jesus. "I am the way," He says, "the truth, and the life" (John 14:6). The Law is not the way to God; Christ is the way.

When Paul wrote to the Ephesians that he was an apostle by the will of God, that was true. But when he wrote to this young preacher

Timothy, he said, "I am an apostle by the commandment of God. He made me an apostle. It is not just because I am in the will of God today that I am an apostle. There was a time when He *commanded* me to be an apostle." I think Paul might have been rather reluctant to become an apostle. I'm sure he could have offered excuses to the Lord as Moses did. He hadn't been with the Lord as the other eleven apostles had been. He never knew Him in the days of His flesh; he knew Him only as the glorified Christ. He said he was unworthy to be an apostle. But the Lord Jesus had said, "I *command* you," and that is the reason Paul could walk into a synagogue or go before a gainsaying audience in Athens, or a group of rotten, corrupt sinners in Corinth, and boldly declare the gospel. He was a soldier under orders, an apostle by commandment—not by commission, but by commandment. No one laid hands on Paul to make him an apostle, but the Lord Jesus personally gave him the authority.

Jeremiah had this same kind of authority. He was a shrinking violet, a retiring sort of person, the man with a broken heart. Yet he stepped out and gave some of the strongest statements that ever came from God. Why could he do that? He was a soldier under orders—under orders from God.

Any man who is going to speak for God today needs to do it with authority or he ought to keep quiet. A man who gets up in the pulpit and says, "If you believe *in a fashion*, I expect that *maybe* you'd be saved if you believe *in a way* on Jesus." Such a wishy-washy man has nothing to say for God at all. Paul was an apostle who spoke with the authority of God.

"God our Saviour"—is God our *Savior*? He certainly is: ". . . God so loved the world, that he gave his only begotten Son . . ." (John 3:16). God provided the sacrifice, and the Lord Jesus is the One who came to this earth and executed it.

"And the Lord Jesus Christ, which is our hope." To say that Christ is our *hope* may seem strange to you, as it is not found often in Scripture. Actually, the only other time you will find it is in Colossians 1:27: ". . . Christ in you, the hope of glory." The Lord Jesus died to save you. He lives to keep you saved. He is going to come someday to take you to be with Himself and to consummate that salvation. He is our faith when we look backwards; He is love when we look around us today; and He is our hope as we look ahead. But it is hope, actually, all the way through our lives, and that hope is anchored in the person of the Lord Jesus Christ.

"Timothy"—sometimes he is called Timothy and sometimes Timotheus. Timotheus is made up of two Greek words which mean "that which is dear to God." Timothy was dear to God, he was dear to the apostle Paul, and he was dear to the local churches.

We read of Timothy in the Books of Acts, Ephesians, and Philippians. His father was a Greek. His grandmother, Lois, and his mother, Eunice, became Christians before him. He lived in Lystra where Paul was stoned. I feel that Paul was actually raised from the dead at that time, and this may have had a lot to do with the conversion of Timothy. As a young man he probably was rather skeptical, and this event may have helped convince him and bring him to conversion. After his conversion he became an avowed follower of Paul.

Timothy was a man who had a good reputation. We read of him in Acts 16:2–5: "Which was well reported of by the brethren that were at Lystra and Iconium. Him would Paul have to go forth with him; and took and circumcised him because of the Jews which were in those quarters: for they knew all that his father was a Greek. And as they went through the cities, they delivered them the decrees for to keep, that were ordained of the apostles and elders which were at Jerusalem. And so were the churches established in the faith, and increased in number daily." As Timothy worked with Paul he became one in whom Paul had the utmost confidence, while others in the churches proved to be false brethren who deceived him.

It is the joy of every pastor to have wonderful friends in his church. I have lived and ministered in Pasadena, California since 1940. I meet people everywhere, some who came to know the Lord as early as 1940 or 1941, who are still following in the Lord's steps, and they are loyal, faithful friends of mine. That is why we keep our ministry's headquarters here, for we have a host of wonderful, trusted friends in this area.

Paul had those whom he couldn't trust, but Timothy was one he could trust. He wrote in Philippians: "But I trust in the Lord Jesus to send Timotheus shortly unto you, that I also may be of good comfort, when I know your state. For I have no man likeminded, who will naturally care for your state. For all seek their own, not the things which are Jesus Christ's. But ye know the proof of him, that, as a son with the father, he hath served with me in the gospel. Him therefore I hope to send presently, so soon as I shall see how it will go with me" (Phil. 2:19-23).

"Timothy, my own son in the faith" could be translated as "my true son in the faith" or "my genuine son in the faith." Paul had led Timothy to the Lord, and they were very close.

"Grace, mercy, and peace, from God our Father and Jesus Christ our Lord." At first this may appear to be the same as the introductions to Paul's other epistles. Yes, Paul has used *grace* and *peace* before, but we have another word here, and that is *mercy*. *Mercy* is a word that was used in the Old Testament and was equivalent to the word *grace*. It was the Old Testament sacrifice that made the holy and righteous and just throne of God into a *mercy* seat.

When you and I come to God, we don't want justice, for we would be condemned. What we want and need from God is mercy. And God has provided mercy for all His creatures. He has all the mercy that you need. Yet His mercy is just like money in the bank which will do you no good unless you write a check, and the check you need to write is the check of faith. God is rich in mercy, but when He saves you, He saves you by His grace. God is merciful to you, and He is merciful to all sinners in the world, even those who blaspheme Him and repudiate Him and turn their back on Him. He sends rain on the just and the unjust—He doesn't play favorites, even with His own people. Sinners today get rich and they prosper. They often seem to do better than God's own people. He is merciful to sinners. But when you come to God, you must come by *faith*—write the check of faith—and then God will save you by His *grace*.

These three words—love, mercy, and grace—are a little trinity. *Love* is that in God which existed before He could care to exercise mercy or grace. God is love; it is His nature, His attribute. *Mercy* is that in God which provided for the need of sinful man. *Grace* then is that in Him which acts freely to save because all the demands of His holiness have been satisfied. Therefore, because God is merciful, you can come to Him, and by His grace He'll save you. You don't have to bring anything, you cannot bring anything, because it would only be filthy rags to God.

A do-gooder is one who thinks he does not need the mercy of God, that his own good works will save him. I knew a man who, although he was on his deathbed, said to me, "Preacher, you don't need to tell me that I need Christ as a Savior and that I need the mercy and the grace of God. I don't need it: I'm willing to stand before Him just like I am." Then he went on to tell me all that he had done in his life. He had been deeply involved with the Community Chest and with an orphans' home and on and on. Oh, he was a do-gooder, and he was going to stand before God on that! My friend, a do-good salvation will not do you any good when you really need it. The salvation God provides will enable you to do good, the kind of good which is acceptable to Him. The righteousness of man is filthy rags in His sight.

So we have found that Paul uses here (and throughout all of the Pastoral Epistles) expressions that we will not see elsewhere in his writings. He obviously spoke to these young preachers in an intimate and more personal way than he did in his public speaking or writing. Wouldn't you love to have been Timothy, to have traveled with Paul and have the great apostle open his mind and heart to you? Well, my friend, the Spirit of God is here and He is talking to us through this epistle which Paul wrote to Timothy.

Although 1 Timothy is intimate and personal, it has to do with the affairs of the local church, the body of believers as it manifests itself in the community. And I want to say here—perhaps it reveals the pastor in me—that every believer should be identified with some local church.

"God our Father"—God is Paul's Father, He is Timothy's Father, and He is your Father if you have received Christ. He is my Father because I have received Christ and have been brought into the family of God. What a privilege that is! Paul had been a Pharisee, and in Judaism he had never had the privilege of calling God his Father.

"Jesus Christ our Lord." Anything that is done in the local church needs to be done in the name of Christ and at His command. He is the Head of the church; He is the Lord. The Lord Jesus said, "You call Me

Lord, Lord, and yet you don't do the things I say; you don't obey Me."
Could He say the same thing to many of us today? He warned that
there are going to be many at the judgment who will say, "Lord, Lord,
didn't we do this and that, and the other thing? We were as busy as
termites for You!" And He will have to say to them, "I don't even know
you. I didn't know you were doing that in My name, for you certainly
didn't seek My will. You didn't seek to obey Me." We need not only to
call Him Lord but also *obey* Him as Lord.

WARNING AGAINST UNSOUND DOCTRINE

We have said that this epistle deals with the creed and the conduct of
the local church. Your creed must be right before your conduct can be
right. It is almost an impossibility to think wrong and act right. One
time a man complained to me: "When a woman driver puts her hand
out the window at an intersection it means nothing but that the window is open! You never know what she is going to do, because sometimes she signals left and turns right, and sometimes she signals right
and turns left!" It is sad that man often tries to act right even though
his thinking is very wrong. It is impossible to keep that up for very
long, my friend.

> **As I besought thee to abide still at Ephesus, when I went
> into Macedonia, that thou mightest charge some that
> they teach no other doctrine [1 Tim. 1:3].**

"That thou mightest charge some that they teach no other doctrine"—
in other words, that they teach no *different* doctrine. Paul wrote to the
Galatians that there was no other gospel. The Judaizers there were
preaching another gospel, but Paul said there was none other. There is
only one gospel, and there is only one doctrine.

"Doctrine" refers to the teaching of the church. What should be the
teaching of the local church? It should be what it was from the very
beginning. Following the Day of Pentecost it is recorded that "they
continued in the apostles' doctrine." This was one of the four things
which characterized that church: (1) The apostles' doctrine (2) fellow-

ship; (3) prayers; and (4) the breaking of bread, or the Lord's Supper. These are the four "fingerprints" of the visible church. A church is not a true church of Christ if its doctrine is not the apostles' doctrine.

I recognize that our varying interpretations of the Scriptures lead us to disagree on some points of doctrine. I had lunch one time with a very fine, outstanding Pentecostal preacher here in Southern California. We talked over what we agreed on and what we disagreed on, and it was not as severe a difference as some might think. As we concluded he said to me, "Dr. McGee, we agree on so much, and we agree on what is basic; therefore we ought not to fall out on the things that actually are not essential things." I was glad he felt that way. I am sorry everybody doesn't believe like I do, but there are some who don't.

However, we must hold to the apostles' doctrine, the basic truths of the faith. The apostles taught the plenary, verbal inspiration of the Scriptures, the integrity and inerrancy of the Word of God. And they taught the deity of Christ. We will see in this very epistle that Paul had anexalted view of the Lord Jesus Christ. There are those who say he did not teach the deity of Christ. Well, of all things, that is one thing on which Paul is as clear as the noonday sun. He clearly taught the deity of Christ. Even here in this chapter when he says, "God our Father and Jesus Christ our Lord," he places Christ right beside God, making it clear that He is God.

"I besought thee to abide still at Ephesus." Paul had left Timothy in Ephesus while he himself was in Macedonia. Ephesus was a very important city, and Paul had spent more time there than anywhere else and had his greatest ministry there. Timothy was to remind the Ephesians to teach no other doctrine. If the teaching of the church is not right, it is not a church. It does not matter how many deacons, elders, pastors, song leaders, choirs, or Sunday schools it might have. If the doctrine is not there, it is not a church. The doctrine must be that of the apostles.

Neither give heed to fables and endless genealogies, which minister questions, rather than godly edifying which is in faith: so do [1 Tim. 1:4].

"Neither give heed to fables," or do not give heed to myths. Ephesus was the heartland of the mystery religions of that day. In that great center there was the temple to Hadrian, the temple to Trajan, and the great temple of Diana. All of that centered in Ephesus. These were all based on the mythology of the Greeks, and the Ephesian believers were to shun them.

Paul's reference to "fables" or myths could possibly mean the philosophy of Philo. Philo was an outstanding and brilliant Israelite who took the Old Testament and spiritualized it. In other words, he attempted to introduce the myth viewpoint. We have some of this same teaching in our old-line denominational seminaries today. They teach, for example, that the Book of Genesis is a myth, that the stories there are myths and the men didn't actually live. There is such an accumulation of evidence to support the Book of Genesis from the recent findings of archaeology that the liberals seem to have backed down from this teaching somewhat.

"Endless genealogies." This could refer to the false teaching that the church is just a continuation of Judaism, that it is just one genealogy following another and not a matter of God dealing with man in different dispensations. Such teaching leads to great confusion as to the positions of Israel and the church in God's program.

Also the Greeks were teaching at that time what was known as the demiurge, and this teaching became a part of the first heresy within the church, which was Gnosticism. They taught that there were emanations from a divine center. The original created a being, and that being created another being below him, and he created another, and then another, and so on down the line. They wanted to fit Jesus in somewhere along that line as one of the created beings.

"Which minister questions, rather than godly edifying which is in faith." In other words, Paul tells Timothy that all these types of false teaching won't build you up in the faith. I think we can observe today in the liberal churches the fruit of their many years of unbelief. It has produced a hard core of almost heartless individuals who absolutely lack faith. They have rejected the Word of God, and the results we see in their churches are unbelievable.

> **Now the end of the commandment is charity out of a pure heart, and of a good conscience, and a faith unfeigned [1 Tim. 1:5].**

"Charity [love] out of a pure heart." Paul again is using intimate expressions in writing to this young preacher that you will not find in his epistles to the churches. He tells Timothy that what is taught in the church should produce love out of a pure heart. A "pure heart" is in contrast to our old nature. It means a person who has been made righteous in Christ and can now manifest the fruit of the Spirit, which includes love.

There are three things that should be manifest in the church. The first is faith—faith in God and in His Word. The second is love. Love is not something you simply mouth all the time. Love is an active concern for others, which means you won't gossip about them or in any way bring harm to them.

I know of one church that has done everything it can to wreck the ministry of its pastor. The one thing they aren't justified in saying is that he didn't teach the Word of God—he did teach it. Yet they had accused him of not having taught it. And at the same time they talk about love. What hypocrisy! Love is not something you just talk about; it is something that must be made manifest.

Faith should be lived out in the life of a church, and love should be lived out. You do need an organization and church officers, but whether you have an episcopal or congregational or presbyterian form of government does not make much difference. If faith and love are lacking, you have nothing more than a lodge, a religious club of some sort. But if faith and love are manifest, the form of government is not too important.

The third thing that should be manifest in the life of a church is "a good conscience." I do not believe that conscience is a good guide even for a believer; yet a believer ought to have a good conscience. When you lie down at night, do you feel bad about something you've said or done during the day? Many sensitive Christians are like that. I had a call one time from a person who was weeping and said, "I said something about you that I should not have, and I hope you'll forgive me." I hadn't known anything about it, by the way, but apparently he hadn't been able to sleep that night because of it. It is good to have a sensitive conscience. Many have consciences that have been seared with a hot iron; that is, they are insensitive to right or wrong.

These three wonderful graces—love, a good conscience, and faith—are the things Paul says should be manifested by believers in a local church.

From which some having swerved have turned aside unto vain jangling [1 Tim. 1:6].

"Vain jangling" means empty chatter, beautiful words, flowery language. There are people who will butter you up and pat you on the back, but it means nothing. It's all just talk.

Desiring to be teachers of the law; understanding neither what they say, nor whereof they affirm [1 Tim. 1:7].

Paul is really laying it on the line. He makes it clear there are those who teach error, and they do it with assurance. They reject the Word of God and actually do not understand what they are talking about.

But we know that the law is good, if a man use it lawfully [1 Tim. 1:8].

In this section where Paul is warning believers against unsound doctrine, he has mentioned the mystery religions and the idolatry that abounded in Ephesus where young Timothy was. He has also warned against the false teaching that sought to make the Old Testament merely a mythology. Now Paul warns against legalists, those who taught that the law is a means of salvation and a means of sanctification after salvation.

The Law served a purpose, but God did not give it as a means of salvation. The Law condemns us; it reveals to man that he is a sinner in need of a Savior. Under the Law the best man in the world is absolutely condemned, but under the gospel the worst man can be justified if he will believe in Christ.

The sinner cannot be saved by good works for he is unable to perform any good works. Paul wrote in Romans, "So then they that are in the flesh cannot please God" (Rom. 8:8). This idea that in and of yourself you can please God absolutely contradicts the Word of God. It is impossible to please Him—you *cannot* meet His standard.

Good works cannot produce salvation, but salvation can produce good works. We are not saved *by* good works, but we are saved *unto* good works. Paul makes this very clear in Ephesians 2:8–10 where we read: "For by grace are ye saved through faith; and that not of yourselves: it is the gift of God: Not of works, lest any man should boast. For we are his workmanship, created in Christ Jesus unto good works, which God hath before ordained that we should walk in them."

"We know that the law is good, if a man use it lawfully." The Law reveals the will of God—it is morally excellent. It is good for moral conduct but not for obtaining salvation. It cannot save a sinner, but it can correct him or reveal that he is a sinner. *That* is its purpose.

> **Knowing this, that the law is not made for a righteous man, but for the lawless and disobedient, for the ungodly and for sinners, for unholy and profane, for murderers of fathers, and murderers of mothers, for manslayers,**
>
> **For whoremongers, for them that defile themselves with mankind, for mensteaIers, for liars, for perjured persons, and if there be any other thing that is contrary to sound doctrine [1 Tim. 1:9–10].**

The Law was not given to the righteous man, the one who has been made righteous because of his faith in Christ. That man has been called to a much higher plane before God. The Law was given for the lawless. "Thou shalt not kill" is not given to the child of God who has no thought of murdering anyone, who does not want to hurt anyone but wants to help. That commandment was given to the man who is a murderer at heart. It is given to control the natural man. The Law is "for whoremongers, for them that defile themselves with mankind, for menstealers, for liars, for perjured persons." Those who have come to Christ were not saved by the Law, but by the grace of God. They have been brought to a plane of living higher even than that given in the Law.

Let me give two illustrations of this that I trust will be helpful. Imagine a judge on a bench who has a lawbreaker brought before him. He is guilty, and he should pay a heavy fine and go to prison. However, the judge says, "I have a son who loves this prisoner although he has broken the law and I must condemn him. My son is a wealthy man and has agreed to pay his fine. He's also agreed to go to prison on behalf of this man. Therefore, his penalty has been fully paid. I am going to take this criminal into my home, and I am going to treat him as a son of mine." When the judge takes the criminal into his home, he no longer says things like, "Thou shalt not kill" or "Thou shalt not steal" (Exod. 20:13, 15). The man is now his son. The judge will talk to him about loving the other members of his family, how he is to conduct himself at the table, treat his wife with respect, and take part in the family chores. You see, this man is treated on an altogether different basis from what he was before. That is what God has done for the believing sinner. We are above and beyond the law. The law is for that fellow out yonder who is a lawbreaker. It is given to control the old nature, the flesh.

The other illustration is one that Dr. Harry Ironside told me years ago. After teaching at an Indian conference in Flagstaff, Arizona, Dr. Ironside took one of the Christian Indians with him to Oakland, California. Among other things, this Indian was asked to speak at a young people's group that was mixed up on the ideas of law and grace. They were confused about the place of the law in the Christian life. The Indian told the group, "I came here from Flagstaff on the train, and we stopped over for several hours in Barstow. There in the station's waiting room I noticed signs on the walls which said, 'Do Not Spit on the Floor.' That was the rule there. I looked down on the floor, and observed that nobody had paid any attention to the law. But when we got here to Oakland I was invited to stay in a lovely Christian home. As I sat in the living room I looked around and noticed pretty pictures on the walls, but no signs which said 'Do Not Spit on the Floor.' I got down on my hands and knees and felt the rug and, you know, nobody had spit on the floor. In Barstow it was law, but in the home in which I'm staying it is grace."

Under law man never kept it, he couldn't measure up to it, and he broke it continually. Under grace a man is brought into the family of God, and he is not going to murder or lie. If he does, he is surely out of fellowship with God.

"Any other thing that is contrary to sound doctrine." Paul adds this in case he has left out something. It covers any and all sin he may have omitted in his list.

PERSONAL TESTIMONY OF PAUL

According to the glorious gospel of the blessed God, which was committed to my trust [1 Tim. 1:11].

Again this is one of those unique statements that Paul uses in writing to this young preacher which you will not find in his epistles to the churches. It might be translated: "According to the gospel of glory of the blessed God, which was committed to my trust." Isn't that a wonderful way to speak of it!

And I thank Christ Jesus our Lord, who hath enabled me, for that he counted me faithful, putting me into the ministry [1 Tim. 1:12].

"I thank Christ Jesus our Lord"—Paul emphasizes the Lordship of Christ.

"He counted me faithful, putting me into the ministry." The idea of ministry is greatly misunderstood in our day. All believers are in the ministry; not one of us is out of the ministry if he is a child of God. The word Paul uses here for ministry is the same as the word for deacon, and every believer is a minister of the Lord Jesus Christ.

Paul even calls rulers ministers—"ministers of God." We say that we have voted for a certain man or that the people put a man into his office, but I think that sometimes God overrules who is to be put into office. Rulers are supposed to function as ministers of God.

Paul is grateful to God that He has put him into His service as a missionary. Every believer has some service to perform for the Lord.

Who was before a blasphemer, and a persecutor, and injurious: but I obtained mercy, because I did it ignorantly in unbelief [1 Tim. 1:13].

"Who was before a blasphemer"—Paul uses this awful word and says that he was a blasphemer. He had blasphemed the Lord Jesus, and he had hated Him. I think he was present at the Crucifixion and ridiculed the Lord Jesus. Paul says that he had been a blasphemer, a persecutor, and that he had injured the church.

"But I obtained mercy." When Paul speaks of his salvation he says he was saved by the *grace* of God. It was the *mercy* of God that put him into the ministry.

I have never really figured out why the Lord has used me in this ministry of giving out the Word of God. If you had said to me when I was a young, smart-alecky bank clerk that I was someday going to be in the ministry, I would have said it was absurd. I didn't want it, and I didn't have anything that would commend me to it. But God by His mercy, my friend, has put me into His service, His ministry. He is rich in mercy, and I have used quite a bit of it in my lifetime!

"Because I did it ignorantly in unbelief." This was Paul's condition, and it was the condition of all of us before we came to Christ.

And the grace of our Lord was exceeding abundant with faith and love which is in Christ Jesus [1 Tim. 1:14].

Paul was saved by the grace of God, who brought him to the place of faith and love "which is in Christ Jesus." Again, these are the things that will be manifest in the life of a believer.

This is a faithful saying, and worthy of all acceptation, that Christ Jesus came into the world to save sinners; of whom I am chief [1 Tim. 1:15].

This is a very important verse of Scripture because it affirms that "Christ Jesus came into the world to save sinners." He didn't come to be the greatest teacher the world has ever known, although He was that. He didn't come to set a moral example, but He did do that. He came into the world to save sinners.

When you give your testimony make sure that you don't tell people how wonderful *you* are or all *you* have accomplished. Tell them you were a *sinner* and that *Christ* saved you. That is what is important.

"Of whom I am chief." When Paul says he was the chiefest of sinners, he is not using hyperbole. He is not using high-flung oratory. He is speaking the truth. He was the chief of sinners; he blasphemed the Lord Jesus and shot out his lip at Him.

"But," Paul says, "I've been saved." The Lord Jesus came to save sinners, and if you say, "I don't think Christ can save me—I'm the worst," you are wrong. Paul is the chief of sinners, and the chief of sinners has already been saved. So *you* will be able to be saved if you want to be. The decision rests with you. All you need do is turn to Christ, and He'll do the rest. He is faithful—Paul says, "This is a *faithful* saying."

> **Howbeit for this cause I obtained mercy, that in me first Jesus Christ might shew forth all longsuffering, for a pattern to them which should hereafter believe on him to life everlasting [1 Tim. 1:16].**

"Howbeit for this cause I obtained mercy"—you see, he needed mercy in order to become a minister, to be a missionary.

"That in me first Jesus Christ might shew forth all long-suffering, for a pattern to them which should hereafter believe on him to life everlasting."

Paul said that he was not only a preacher of, but also an example of, the gospel.

> **Now unto the King eternal, immortal, invisible, the only wise God, be honour and glory for ever and ever. Amen [1 Tim. 1:17].**

Paul simply couldn't go any further without sounding out this tremendous doxology. Who is "the King eternal"? He is the Lord Jesus Christ. And who is the Lord Jesus? He is "the only wise God." Don't tell me that Paul did not teach that the Lord Jesus was God. Paul considered Him to be God manifest in the flesh, and here he gives this wonderful testimony to that.

CHARGE TO TIMOTHY

This charge I commit unto thee, son Timothy, according to the prophecies which went before on thee, that thou by them mightest war a good warfare [1 Tim. 1:18].

"This charge I commit unto thee, son Timothy." Although his letter to Timothy is very practical and has to do with the local church and Timothy's responsibilities in it, it also reveals something of the wonderful personal relationship that must have existed between the apostle Paul and Timothy. This is Paul's personal charge to Timothy as a young man in the ministry.

"Son Timothy"—he was Paul's spiritual son; Paul had led him to Christ.

"According to the prophecies which went before on thee." Paul had real spiritual discernment, and evidently God had directed him to take this young man along with him and allow him to have the position which he held in the early church.

"That thou by them mightest war a good warfare." You ought never to fight a war unless your heart is in it, unless you are fighting for a real cause and intend to get the victory. As a Christian, Timothy had a real enemy. He was involved in a spiritual warfare. Paul wanted him to fight a good fight and not to make shipwreck of the faith—as others were doing.

Holding faith, and a good conscience; which some having put away concerning faith have made shipwreck [1 Tim. 1:19].

Living the Christian life is not as simple as some would like us to believe. It is more complex than walking when the light is green and not walking when the light turns red. We have intricate personalities, and Paul is saying there is real danger for us in our human inconsistencies and failures. I assume you are not living in some ivory tower somewhere. Some Christians feel they are, that they are above the landscape and the smog and are way up yonder. But for those of us today who are walking on the sidewalks of our cities and rubbing shoulders with rough humanity and the problems of the world, we find that there are inconsistencies and failures. The danger we face is that of accomodating our faith to our failure.

A man I knew came home from the mission field and got a job doing something rather ordinary. He said, "The Lord led me to do this." He had trained about nine years to be a missionary, and now he said the Lord had led him back home to take a job that just wasn't very important. I asked him if he really felt that that was the way the Lord leads, and he insisted it was. He repeats this so frequently that I am afraid what actually happened was that he accommodated his faith to his human failure on the mission field. That is a grave danger for all of us. My friend, when you and I fail—when there is inconsistency in our lives—we ought to go to Him and tell Him that we have fallen short, that we haven't measured up. As we will read shortly in 1 Timothy, the Lord Jesus is a wonderful mediator between God and man. We need not be afraid to go to Him.

Of whom is Hymenaeus and Alexander; whom I have delivered unto Satan, that they may learn not to blaspheme [1 Tim. 1:20].

"Of whom is Hymenaeus and Alexander"—Paul cites two examples of apostates in his day. He mentions them elsewhere in Scripture, and he doesn't have much good to say about either one of them. In 2 Timothy he writes, "Alexander the coppersmith did me much evil . . ." (2 Tim. 4:14).

"Whom I have delivered unto Satan." These men had failed, they were apostates, and Paul exercised a ministry which I feel only an apostle can exercise. He says, "I have delivered [them] unto Satan." This is not something we could put under the name of ecclesiastical discipline or excommunication today. It is Paul exercising what was his prerogative and position as an apostle; he hands over these men to Satan.

We have another occasion of this mentioned in 1 Corinthians where Paul writes: "For I verily, as absent in body, but present in spirit, have judged already, as though I were present, concerning him that hath so done this deed. In the name of our Lord Jesus Christ, when ye are gathered together, and my spirit, with the power of our Lord Jesus Christ, To deliver such an one unto Satan for the destruction of the flesh, that the spirit may be saved in the day of the Lord Jesus" (1 Cor. 5:3–5). This is an authority the apostles had which we do not have today. We have no right to deliver any man over to Satan, but the apostles did. Peter exercised it also: I imagine that if we could talk to Ananias and Sapphira they would be able to tell us something of his authority as an apostle (see Acts 5:1–11).

CHAPTER 2

THEME: Public prayer and woman's place in the churches

PUBLIC PRAYER

Public prayer is prayer for the public and for public officials.

I exhort therefore, that, first of all, supplications, prayers, intercessions, and giving of thanks, be made for all men;

For kings, and for all that are in authority; that we may lead a quiet and peaceable life in all godliness and honesty [1 Tim. 2:1-2].

Paul says that Christians are to pray for public officials, and I take it that he meant that the prayers were to be made in the church. To bring this up-to-date, he is saying the Democrats ought to pray for the Republicans, and the Republicans ought to pray for the Democrats. Many years ago a famous chaplain of the Senate was asked by a visitor, "Do you pray for the senators?" He replied, "No, I look at the senators, and then I pray for the country!" That is exactly what Paul says we need to do. We need to pray for our country, and we need to pray for those who have authority over us. If you are a Republican and a Democrat is in office, pray for him. If you are a Democrat and a Republican is in office, pray for him.

"For kings." Paul says we are to pray for the kings who rule. You may ask, "Yes, but are we to pray when the government is a corrupt one?" Paul is saying we are to pray even if it's a corrupt government. We are to pray for whoever is in power. Remember that the man who was in power in Rome when Paul wrote was bloody Nero, yet he says we are to pray for kings, whoever they are.

"That we may lead a quiet and peaceable life in all godliness and honesty." Any government is better than no government. Some people may question that, but an evil, corrupt government, if it really governs, is better than anarchy. I agree with those who argue that politics is crooked—man has certainly corrupted and misused political power—but there does remain a semblance of law and order. Civil government is a gift from God, and we ought to give thanks for it and pray for it. Many of us fall short of praying for our government in order that we might continue to live quietly and peaceably.

For this is good and acceptable in the sight of God our Saviour;

Who will have all men to be saved, and to come unto the knowledge of the truth [1 Tim. 2:3–4].

A second reason we should pray for government is in order that the gospel might continue to go out to the lost. I believe that we are actually going to see the persecution of Christians in this country in the future. I do not mean the persecution of church members—the liberal church is so compromised today that they will go along with whatever comes along. I am saying that genuine believers in Christ may encounter persecution. Paul was beginning to experience persecution himself, and he said the believers were to pray for the leaders who were responsible for it. It was "good and acceptable in the sight of God" to pray for these men. Why? Because it is God's will that all men might be saved.

It is not important for you and me to get a certain man elected to office. I have never in my ministry recommended a candidate for office. I am not called to do that, and I don't believe any minister is. I am to pray for our leaders regardless of who they are in order that the gospel can go out. I want a man in office who is going to make it possible for the Word of God to continue to be given to the lost. This should be our concern and our prayer.

For there is one God, and one mediator between God and men, the man Christ Jesus [1 Tim. 2:5].

"For there is one God." The Romans worshiped many gods, and today people worship many gods in a different sort of way. People are giving themselves to many things—some to pleasure, some to entertainment, and so on. The entertainment world, for example, has become a religion of sorts for many people. There are women who would sacrifice their virtue in a moment and men who would sacrifice their honor in order to become a movie or television star. People have many different gods today. But there is only *one God*, and He is the Creator.

"And one mediator between God and men, the man Christ Jesus." In Old Testament times the Israelite went to the temple where there were many priests. He could go to God through them. Paul is saying that now there is only one Mediator to whom we are to go. We are not to go to any human being down here; it is not necessary to go through a minister. There is a Mediator between God and man.

We need a mediator, we need a priest, and we have one, the Great High Priest. Job's heart cry even in his day was, "Neither is there any daysman betwixt us, that might lay his hand upon us both" (Job 9:33). In effect, Job was crying out, "Oh, if there were somebody who could take hold of God's hand and then take hold of my hand and bring us together that there might be communication and understanding between us!"

Well, my friend, today we have a Mediator—the Lord Jesus Christ has come. He has one hand in the hand of Deity because He is *God*. He is able to save to the uttermost because He is God, and He has paid the price for our salvation. He is a Mediator because He has also become *man*. He can hold my hand; He understands me. He understands you; you can go to Him, and He is not going to be upset with you. He will not lose His temper or strike you or hurt you in any way. You may say, "Well, I've failed. I've done such-and-such, and I've come short of the glory of God." My friend, He knows that, and He still loves you and wants to put His arm around you.

Isaiah wrote to the Lord: "In all their affliction he was afflicted . . ." (Isa. 63:9). Some scholars say that this should read, "In all their affliction he was *not* afflicted." Either way you read it, it is wonderful. I think maybe God wants us to see it both ways, but I like it, "In all their affliction he was *not* afflicted." God went through the wilderness with the children of Israel. When they failed and disobeyed at Kadesh-barnea, He didn't say, "Well, good-bye—I'm through with you, you've failed." No, He went with them for forty years. But He also went on ahead: He gave Moses their instructions for living for the time when they would enter the Promised Land. But He waited for them and dealt patiently with them in their time of affliction in the wilderness. He wasn't afflicted; He didn't break down and fail, but just stayed there with them.

He has dealt with me in the same way, and it is wonderful to have such a Mediator through whom we can go to God. And you should go through Him, because there is really no use coming and telling me your troubles. I may not be sympathetic with you; I might not really understand your case. He does. He's human. He is a daysman, a Mediator. He has put His hand in mine. I don't put my hand in His; He puts *His* hand in mine. That is the wonder of it all! He has come down and put His hand in mine and taken hold of me, but He also holds on to God because He is God, and He has brought us together.

This Mediator is the One the world needs to know because there is but *one* way to salvation. Peter said to the religious leaders of his day: "Neither is there salvation in any other: for there is none other name under heaven given among men, whereby we must be saved" (Acts 4:12). Christ is the only way, but the tremendous thing is that He *will* bring you right through to God if you will turn to Him.

One time while in Canada I was told that I needed to get onto a certain freeway to get to Detroit, Michigan, but if I missed that freeway I was in real trouble. It took a great deal of manipulating around, but once I managed to find that freeway it brought me right into Detroit. I was thankful for the man who had said, "There is only one way." I am also thankful that I have been told there is one way to God, one Mediator. He is the only One who can bring us together: He can bring us to God because He is God and He is also a man, "the man Christ Jesus."

Who gave himself a ransom for all, to be testified in due time [1 Tim. 2:6].

"Ransom" is *antilutron* in the Greek, and it means a "redemption price." Christ paid a price for our redemption. We needed to be redeemed—you and I were lost sinners, and He was the ransom.

Whereunto I am ordained a preacher, and an apostle, (I speak the truth in Christ, and lie not;) a teacher of the Gentiles in faith and verity [1 Tim. 2:7].

"I am ordained" might be better translated "I am appointed." Paul says that he was appointed a preacher and an apostle.

"Preacher" comes from the Greek word *kerux*, which means "a herald or a trumpet," referring to one who gives out the gospel. He has been appointed one to declare the gospel.

"(I speak the truth in Christ, and lie not;)." It might seem strange to you that Paul would say this to a young preacher who is his personal friend. I think he is saying it to encourage him—Timothy knows it is true.

"A teacher of the Gentiles in faith and verity [truth]." Again this is something that he did not write to the churches. He has always said that he is an apostle of the Gentiles; here he says that he is not only the apostle to give the gospel, but he is also the one to *teach* the Gentiles.

HOW MEN ARE TO PRAY

I will therefore that men pray every where, lifting up holy hands, without wrath and doubting [1 Tim. 2:8].

"I will"—Paul is not making this a matter of his will, but is saying, "I desire."

"That men pray every where"—that is, in every place where believers meet. Paul is talking about *public* prayer, prayer in the public service.

"Lifting up holy hands." This was a custom practiced in the early church. It revealed the dedication in the lives of those praying.

Now there are those who lift up their hands in services today, and they are sometimes criticized for it. There is nothing wrong with lifting up your hands if it is something you feel you want to do. Personally, I have always hesitated to do it because I'm not too sure about my hands, wether they are clean or not, clean physically or otherwise. Notice that Paul says, "holy hands." This would mean that they are hands dedicated to God's service. My friend, you ought not to poke up your hands in a meeting if those hands are not used for the service of Christ.

"Without wrath"—all sins have been confessed. You don't come in prayer with anger in your heart, or a bitter spirit, but with all your sins confessed.

"Without . . . doubting." In Hebrews 11:6 we read: "But without faith it is impossible to please him; for he that cometh to God must believe that he is, and that he is a rewarder of them that diligently seek him." When we come to God in prayer, we are to come in faith. One of the reasons I feel that our prayer meetings are not better attended today is that people lack faith. They do not believe that God is going to hear and answer prayer.

I do not mean to be irreverent, but I sometimes think that the Lord must yawn during our prayer meetings because they are so boresome. Prayer should be made in our public services by those who have their sins confessed, who come without bitterness in their hearts, and who come in faith, believing that God will hear and answer. It is this kind of prayer that will make a prayer meeting what it ought to be.

HOW WOMEN ARE TO PRAY

Paul has given the way that men ought to pray, and now he will say how women are to pray. This passage will also touch on the matter of women's dress and their place in the local church.

We live in a day when there are two extreme positions relative to the place women should occupy in the local and visible church. Both positions use this passage of Scripture to support their stand.

One position permits women to occupy a place of prominence and leadership in all public services. They have women preachers, choir directors, and officers. No position is withheld from them and, as a result, the women are not only prominent but we find that they become dominant in the church.

When I was a pastor in Nashville, Tennessee, a tent was put up across the street from my church. The Baptist preacher in town was a good friend of mine and together we went over to meet the husband

and wife team who were going to hold meetings. The wife did the preaching, and the husband did all the leg work. We watched him putting up the tent and setting out the benches and all that sort of thing. He also led the singing. That's all right if you like it that way, but I don't. However, the Baptist preacher and I gave the meetings all the support we could, because they had good meetings and she did preach the gospel. This is an example of the fact that God has used some of these groups who have women preachers in a definite way; but I think, frankly, that He has used them in spite of, not because of, the position of women among them.

The other extreme position on this issue is taken by those who do not allow women any place at all in their public services. You never hear the voice of a woman in public in their meetings, not even in singing. I have had opportunity for good ministry among some of these folk, but believe me, they push their women to the background. I fear that they lose a great deal of talent and that the women could make a marvelous contribution if they were permitted to do so.

To illustrate this, allow me to tell you a story, and I hope you understand that I do so in a facetious manner. There is a little town in the Midwest where there lived a very prominent maiden lady. Everyone agreed that she would have made some man a wonderful wife, but she had never been asked and she died an old maid. The society editor for the local newspaper who normally would cover such a story was out of town, and the sports editor was asked to write up a little notice of this lady's death. He concluded the article with these words:

> Here lie the bones of Nancy Jones:
> For her, life held no terrors.
> She lived an old maid, she died an old maid:
> No hits, no runs, no errors.

Churches miss something when they will not use the talent of their women. God can and will use them in His work.

The confusion that exists about this rather practical issue has been brought about by a misunderstanding of this passage of Scripture and also by an unfamiliarity with the Roman world of Paul's day.

Let's establish first that God *has* used women. In the Word of God we see Deborah, Queen Esther, Ruth, and others. In church history, we find women like Mary Fletcher and Priscilla Gurney. There are multitudes of others whom God has used in a wonderful way.

However, in the Roman world the female principle was a part of all the heathen religions, and women occupied a prominent place. The worship of Aphrodite at Corinth was probably one of the most immoral in which prostitution was actually made into a religion. The thousand vestal virgins who were in the temple of Aphrodite on top of the Acropolis there in Corinth were nothing in the world but prostitutes. They were characterized by very disheveled hair. The reason God said that a woman should have her head covered was so she would not be associated at all with religions like this. Also, in Ephesus where Timothy was at this time, women occupied a very prominent position in the worship at the temple of Diana. In all the mystery religions there were priestesses. It is because of these heathen practices that Paul is emphasizing in this passage that this matter of sex is not to enter into the public prayer in the services of the Christian churches. We need to approach this passage with these factors in mind.

In like manner also, that women adorn themselves in modest apparel, with shamefacedness and sobriety; not with broided hair, or gold, or pearls, or costly array;

But (which becometh women professing godliness) with good works [1 Tim. 2:9–10].

"In like manner also"—Paul has said how men are to pray in public, and now he will say how women are to pray. Note that he is saying women *are* to pray. That is not the issue, but he is telling them the *way* in which they are to pray in public. His emphasis will be upon inner adornment rather than outward adornment. Women are to pray in public, but they should not dress up from the viewpoint of appealing to God in a sexual or physical way.

I want to make it very clear that I feel that a woman should dress as nicely as she possibly can. There is nothing wrong with a woman dressing in a way that is appealing to her husband (or, if she is single, to a man). I have made this statement before, and one lady wrote me in reaction to it:

> I never thought I'd see the day when I would feel a need to take you to task over anything. Usually I agree with you on everything that you say. But on Friday morning in your last study in Proverbs, I guess you hit a raw nerve. You were admonishing young men on choosing a wife, and you said, "First of all, make sure she's a Christian." I agree with that. Then you said, "And if possible, choose a pretty one." Really, Dr. McGee, do you think that's quite fair? After all, there are far more plain, ordinary-looking girls and women than really pretty ones, and pray tell, where would they be if men chose only pretty ones? I happen to be one of those plain, ordinary-looking women, and I'm so glad my husband didn't choose one of the pretty ones, or I'd have missed out on twenty-five years of happy married life. I'm not really angry with you. How could I be when you've taught me so much of the deep truths of God's Word? I just wanted you to know that I think you ought to say a little something for us women whom the Lord did not choose to bless with physical beauty.

I want to say something to that woman and to others: Have you ever stopped to realize that when your husband fell in love with you he thought you were beautiful? Yes, he did. I shall never forget the night that I met my wife. It was a summer night in Texas, and we were invited to the home of mutual friends for dinner. Frankly, these friends were tying to bring us together. I didn't want to go because I had an engagement in Fort Worth that night. My wife didn't want to go because she was going with another fellow! But that night when I saw her—I never shall forget her dark hair, her brown eyes—there in the candlelight I looked at her, and I fell in love with her. I proposed to her on our second date, and the reason I didn't propose on that first date was that I didn't want her to think I was in a hurry! She'd never won a beauty contest, but she was beautiful. How wonderful it was!

I have a notion your husband thought you were beautiful also, and there is nothing wrong in dressing in a way to be attractive to him. But when you go to God in prayer, you don't need that outward adornment. You need that inward adornment. When a woman is going to sing in church, to speak or to have any part in a church service, she ought to keep in mind that her appeal should in no way be on the basis of sex. She should seek to please God, and there is no way in which she can appeal to Him on the basis of sex at all. Such appeal characterized the pagan religions in the Roman world, and Paul is stressing that it should not be a part of the public services of the Christian churches.

Let the woman learn in silence with all subjection.

But I suffer not a woman to teach, nor to usurp authority over the man, but to be in silence [1 Tim. 2:11–12].

These verses have to do with the learning and teaching of doctrine. Keep in mind that the women led in the mystery religions of Paul's day, and they were sex orgies. Paul is cautioning women not to sepak publicly with the idea of making an appeal on the basis of sex. Paul strictly forbade women to speak in tongues in 1 Corinthians 14:34.

For Adam was first formed, then Eve.

And Adam was not deceived, but the woman being deceived was in the transgression.

Notwithstanding she shall be saved in childbearing, if they continue in faith and charity and holiness with sobriety [1 Tim. 2:13–15].

It was the sin of Eve that brought sin into the world. Now every time a woman bears a child, she brings a *sinner* into the world—that is all she can bring into the world. But Mary brought the Lord Jesus, the Savior into the world. So how are women saved? By childbearing—

because Mary brought the Savior into the world. Don't ever say that woman brought sin into the world, unless you are prepared to add that woman also brought the Savior into the world. My friend, no *man* provided a Savior: a *woman* did. However, each individual woman is saved by faith, the same as each man is saved by faith. She is to grow in love and holiness just as a man is.

CHAPTER 3

THEME: Officers in the churches

REQUIREMENTS OF ELDERS

This is a true saying, If a man desire the office of a bishop, he desireth a good work [1 Tim. 3:1].

"This is a *true* saying" could be translated, "This is a *faithful* saying." In other words, this is a saying that stands the test of time; it is one you can depend upon.

"If a man *desire* the office of a bishop" means if a man *seeks* the office of a bishop. This has in it the thought that there will be the active seeking of the office. I believe that a man who has the qualifications ought to seek the office. He ought to want a place where he can use the gift that the Spirit of God has given him. If the Spirit of God has not given him the gift and is not leading him, then it would be a tragedy indeed if a man sought the office of bishop. This also suggests that there was not just one bishop in the church, but there were several.

"The office of a bishop." *Bishop* is a word that has been misinterpreted and interpreted differently by different groups. Those who practice the episcopal form of church government put great emphasis upon this word and its interpretation.

Bishop actually means "an overseer, a superintendent." In the early church the pastor was called by several different titles: (1) he was called a presbyter, or elder; (2) he was called a pastor, or shepherd; (3) he was called a bishop, or an overseer; and (4) he was called a minister. The pastor was never called "reverend," and I don't think any preacher should be so called. *Reverend* means "terrible, that which incites terror." It is a name which applies only to God.

I take the position that the terms *elder* and *bishop* refer to the same person. Those who hold to the episcopal form of church government will, of course, disagree with me altogether. I believe that the use of "elder" (*presbuteros* in the Greek) refers to the *person* who holds the office, and it suggests that he must be a mature Christian. On the other hand, the use of "bishop" (*episkopos* in the Greek) refers to the *office* that is held. Therefore, these two words apply to the same individual or office.

A bishop in the early church never had authority over other bishops or elders. He did not have authority over churches. You do not find such a practice presented in the Word of God. Even Paul, who founded a number of churches, never spoke of himself as the bishop of a church, or as the one who was ruling a church in any way whatsoever. Therefore, the minister is one who is to serve the church, not rule over it.

"He desireth a good work"—he is seeking a place where he can serve in the church.

> **A bishop then must be blameless, the husband of one wife, vigilant, sober, of good behaviour, given to hospitality, apt to teach [1 Tim. 3:2].**

We have given here the positive requirements of an elder—the things he *ought* to be.

"Blameless." The thing that must be understood is that you *will* be blamed for things if you hold an office, any office, in the church. What is important is that the accusation must not be true. An elder must be blameless in the sense that he will not be found guilty of anything of which he might be accused.

Shortly after I had been called to a pastorate in downtown Los Angeles, I met Dr. James McGinley in Chicago. He asked me, "How do you like being pastor in that great church?" "Well," I said, "it's a marvelous opportunity, but I find myself in a very unique place: I am accused of many things, and I can't defend myself. You cannot spend all your time answering everybody, so I've determined to just preach the Word of God and not try to answer them." Dr. McGinley said, "Just rejoice that the things you are accused of are not true." It is nice to be in that position, and that should be the position of a bishop—blameless: accused, but not guilty.

"The husband of one wife." This can be interpreted two ways. It could mean that he ought to be married. I feel that Paul had this in mind. You may say, "Well, Paul was not married." I take the position that Paul had been married and his wife had died. He could not have been a member of the Sanhedrin without being married. He simply had not married again, perhaps because of his travels as an apostle.

When I first became a pastor I was not married and I was frequently kidded by a friend who said I had no right to be a pastor if I wasn't married. Using this verse, he would say, "You should be the husband of one wife." However, I think that the primary meaning here is that the bishop or elder should not have *two* wives. Polygamy was common in Paul's day, and bigamy was certainly prevalent. The officer in the church should be the husband of one wife.

"Vigilant" means temperate. The elder should be calm and not credulous. He should be a man who knows how to keep his cool.

"Sober" means sober-minded or serious. He means business. This does not mean an elder cannot have a sense of humor, but he should be serious about the office which he holds.

"Of good behaviour." An elder should be orderly in his conduct. He doesn't do questionable things. I knew a minister who got himself into a great deal of difficulty because of his careless actions. The rumors were that he had had an affair with a woman in his congregation. I'm confident from all the information that came to me from several sources that he was not guilty, but he certainly had been careless in his conduct. He was a young minister, and often at church social gatherings, he would kiddingly say that he was going to take another man's wife home. He would take her, leave her off at her door, and then go on to his home. All this was done with a great deal of kidding, but it caused some people to raise their eyebrows and start talking. My feeling is that the conduct of an officer or a minister should be absolutely above reproach. Kidding is fine, but it should not lead to questionable activity.

"Given to hospitality" means that an elder is to be a hospitable individual. He is the type of fellow who invites his preacher or others out to lunch. I've always liked fellows like that and have had the privilege in recent years of meeting many wonderful and hospitable laymen in my travels all over the country. One will come and put his arm around me and say, "Now can I help you in some way? Is there anything I can do?" They do things like having a bowl of fruit or a bouquet of flowers sent to my hotel room where I happen to be staying. One time in San Diego I broke off a capped tooth, and a doctor friend recommended a dentist there. That dentist is such a wonderful man I still go all the way to San Diego for my dental care. Such hospitable men can be found all across our country.

"Apt to teach." This is something I emphasize, because I do not feel any man ought to be an elder in a church unless he can teach the Word of God. I used to say to my church officers that I wished it was possible to give a theological exam to each one of them to determine if he was qualified to be an officer. I never actually did that, but I always thought it would be a good idea.

Not given to wine, no striker, not greedy of filthy lucre; but patient, not a brawler, not covetous [1 Tim. 3:3].

Now we come to the negative qualifications—the things an elder should *not* be.

"Not given to wine"—he should not be a drunkard.

"No striker"—not violent or pugnacious.

"Not greedy of filthy lucre." He shouldn't have a love of money. The love of money is a root of all evil we are told in Scripture (1 Tim. 6:10). The way a church officer handles his money can lead him into a great deal of trouble—either his own money or the church's money.

"Patient" means reasonable. He should be a reasonable man, someone you can talk to or reason with.

"Not a brawler." He should not be a contentious person. Men who are constantly stirring up trouble in a church should never be selected as church officers.

"Not covetous" again refers to the love of money, but it also suggests idolatry, actually the worship of money. He should not be a man who puts the pursuit of wealth above everything else.

One that ruleth well his own house, having his children in subjection with all gravity [1 Tim. 3:4].

An elder should have the authority in his own home—without being a dictator.

(For if a man know not how to rule his own house, how shall he take care of the church of God?) [1 Tim. 3:5].

A man does not know how to rule the house of God if he cannot rule his own home.

Not a novice, lest being lifted up with pride he fall into the condemnation of the devil [1 Tim. 3:6].

"Not a novice" means not a recent convert, not someone who has recently been saved. Sometimes a man is converted one week, and the next week he is made a church officer or asked to give his testimony. He is not ready for it. This is a caution that needs to be heeded today.

I had the privilege for several years of teaching a Bible study group of Christians in Hollywood. It was natural for them to want to push to the front some prominent personality who had recently made a decision for Christ. However, the cause of Christ is hurt when those who are young in the faith attempt to speak on matters of doctrine about which they are not knowledgeable.

"Lest being lifted up with pride he fall into the condemnation of the devil." Pride was the Devil's great sin. Also it is often the sin of officers in the church and of preachers. It is a danger for all of us, but it is reprehensible when it is in the church.

Moreover he must have a good report of them which are without; lest he fall into reproach and the snare of the devil [1 Tim. 3:7].

"Them which are without" means those who are outside the church. In other words, if a man has a bad reputation on the outside—if he doesn't pay his bills, is untrustworthy, or is a liar—he immediately is *not* a candidate to be an officer in the church. If he is such a man he is really a candidate of the Devil—he would better represent the Devil than he would represent the cause of Christ.

REQUIREMENTS OF DEACONS

Likewise must the deacons be grave, not double-tongued, not given to much wine, not greedy of filthy lucre [1 Tim. 3:8].

The word that is translated "deacon" here is the same word that is sometimes translated as "minister." Paul and Apollos are called deacons. The Lord Jesus is called a minister in Matthew 20:28. In Romans 13:4 government officials are called ministers, and in 2 Corinthians 11:15 ministers of Satan have the word applied to them. *Deacon* or *minister*, therefore, is a general term for a servant or a worker.

We think of the account in Acts 6 as giving the occasion when the office of deacon began in the early church. However, the Greek word for *deacon* is not even used there. But I'm confident we have scriptural grounds to say that those men were being appointed as deacons in the church.

A deacon, although he deals with the material matters of the church, should be a *spiritual* man. We have a problem today when we appoint a man as a deacon on the basis of physical rather than spiritual qualifications. We think that because a man is a successful businessman he will make a good deacon. There are too many men who are appointed to office on that basis.

I have attempted to emphasize in 1 Timothy that the local church is an organization that needs to make itself manifest in the community, and in doing so it gets right down where the rubber meets the road. It must deal with the problems of a building, supplying heat and light, and a lot of material issues that don't seem very romantic. However, the important matter is still that a church is to have a *spiritual* ministry in the community. We often put the material qualifications first, but the men who are in office must have the spiritual qualifications for their office. Someone has put it like this: "When a church ceases to be in touch with another world, she is no longer in touch with this one." I agree with that 100 percent. Until the spiritual aspects are emphasized, a church cannot accomplish the material and practical functions down here. The deacons, therefore, are to have certain spiritual qualifications.

"Grave"—he should be a man of dignity.

"Not double-tongued." A deacon should not be two-faced. A man's word should amount to something. It can be dangerous when a man tries to please everybody or doesn't have the courage to stand on his own two feet. There is a fine balance between being a Mr. Milquetoast and being a dictator. An officer in the church needs to be somewhere between those two.

"Not given to much wine." I take this just as it is: the Bible teaches temperance, and that is important to see. I do not think the Bible teaches total abstinence because there weren't many medicines in those days and wine was used as medicine. In 1 Timothy 5:23 Paul encourages Timothy to use a little wine for his stomach's sake. Even today many of the medicines we take contain a high percentage of alcohol.

The problem we encounter with alcohol in our day is the way it is used as a beverage, and I feel that the church should teach total abstinence because the abuse of alcohol is so prevalent. I do not believe that a Christian should use alcohol as a refreshment or a drink.

"Not greedy of filthy lucre." This means that a deacon should not have an insatiable love of money. He should be a man of integrity and should handle the money of the church in an honest way. There is nothing that can hurt a church more than the accusation that the deacons are juggling the finances. Money given to a church for a specific cause needs to be carefully alloted to the intended cause.

I have discovered in my experience in the ministry that most of the churches I know are run by men of high integrity, but it is that small minority of dishonest men who are muddying the waters and causing difficulty. If there is one thing a church ought to be able to present to the world it is the fact that it is honest and holds a place of high integrity in financial matters.

Holding the mystery of the faith in a pure conscience [1 Tim. 3:9].

"The mystery of the faith" means the revelation of the gospel of Christ. When Paul says "*the* faith" he is not speaking of the abstract quality of faith, but of the doctrines of the faith. He speaks of it as a "mystery" because these doctrines were not revealed in the Old Testament but are now revealed in the New Testament. We are told in Acts that the early church "continued in the apostles' doctrine." The apostles' doctrine was "the faith" of the early church. It should be the faith of the church today, and the church needs to represent that faith before the world.

There are a great many people who think the faith is outmoded and needs to be changed. An editorial in one of our national magazines a number of years ago supported this idea by suggesting an updated list of the "seven deadly sins." Their new list included selfishness, intolerance, indifference, cruelty, violence, and destructiveness. The list replaced lust, of course, with prudery. Lust was replaced, they said, because it had become as commonplace as the neighborhood newsstand or cinema. Gluttony was not included because it was considered a cholesterol problem but not a theological one. Words like *covetousness* and *sloth* were deemed antiquated. The article noted that different segments of society have different concepts of what constitutes sin. For example, young people would have placed irrelevance and hypocrisy high on their list of sins, but destructiveness would not have been included unless it meant only destructiveness of the environment. Similarly, elderly people would want noise, hair, and incivility included on their list. Some would argue that the new list simply contained old sins under new names. For example, selfishness had merely replaced covetousness. The article contended that the old names were obsolete and needed changing if sin was to retain any contemporary, moral force at all. It concluded by affirming that sin is a concept well worth saving!

I would emphatically agree that sin is a concept worth saving, but I must insist also that sin has in no way changed. What the Bible calls sin is still sin. Human nature is still human nature. The spiritual qualifications which the Bible lays down for church officers must still hold good today if the church is to represent the Lord Jesus Christ here on this earth. The church and its officers must hold to New Testament doctrine, calling sin the sins which are clearly labeled as such in the Word of God.

"In a pure conscience"—not with the conscience that has been seared with a hot iron (see 1 Tim. 4:2).

And let these also first be proved; then let them use the office of a deacon, being found blameless [1 Tim. 3:10].

A man should not be shoved into office a month after he joins a church and before he has proved that he is the type of man that Scripture has described here.

Now Paul has a word about the wives of deacons. They must measure up to certain standards also.

Even so must their wives be grave, not slanderers, sober, faithful in all things [1 Tim. 3:11].

"Grave"—they should be serious, able to be calm and cool.

"Not slanderers" means they are not to be gossips. A gossipy deacon's wife can cause much trouble in the church.

"Sober," again, is sober-minded.

"Faithful in all things." She should be faithful to her husband, to Christ Himself, and to His cause.

Let the deacons be the husbands of one wife, ruling their children and their own houses well [1 Tim. 3:12].

For they that have used the office of a deacon well purchase to themselves a good degree, and great boldness in the faith which is in Christ Jesus [1 Tim. 3:13].

The deacons are to meet the same personal and family requirements that were given for the elders.

"Good degree" could be read "good standing." In other words, a deacon who serves well will become known as a man who is to be trusted.

"Boldness" means confidence and courage in witnessing. Remember that a deacon primarily has a *spiritual* office. I remember the case of one man who was a deacon and was asked to take the office of an elder. Well, he didn't think he was spiritual enough or knew the Bible well enough to be an elder. If that was true, then he should not have been a deacon either, but he had been selected a deacon because he was a successful businessman. The spiritual requirements should be met by both elders and deacons before they are allowed to represent the church of Christ.

REPORT OF PAUL TO TIMOTHY

These things write I unto thee, hoping to come unto thee shortly [1 Tim. 3:14].

Paul was in Macedonia, and Timothy was in Ephesus. Paul was hoping to be able to join Timothy shortly.

But if I tarry long, that thou mayest know how thou oughtest to behave thyself in the house of God, which is the church of the living God, the pillar and ground of the truth [1 Tim. 3:15].

I have selected this as the key verse of this epistle because 1 Timothy is a book about church order. While he is away Paul writes, "I've written this to you so you will know how to act in the house of God."

"The church of the living God"—Paul is speaking to the church that *is* the church.

"The pillar and ground of the truth." "Pillar" means the stay, the prop, or that which is foundational. What Paul is saying is that the church is the pillar, the bedrock—it is the prop and support of the truth. If the officers do not represent the truth, the church has no foundation, no prop, and it cannot hold up the truth of God.

Some men purport to represent the truth, but they actually do not represent the truth in the way they lead their lives. I knew a deacon once who carried the biggest Bible I have ever seen. Every time you saw him he was weighed down on one side carrying that Bible. But he was a man you couldn't depend upon—there was a question about his integrity. He hurt the church he served and brought it into disrepute. Paul is writing to tell the church how it should act so that it can represent and proclaim the truth of God to the world on the outside.

And without controversy great is the mystery of godliness: God was manifest in the flesh, justified in the Spirit, seen of angels, preached unto the Gentiles, believed on in the world, received up into glory [1 Tim. 3:16].

This verse probably constitutes one of the earliest creeds of the church. Some think that it was one of the songs of the early church.

"Without controversy"—means confessedly, or obviously.

"Great is the mystery of godliness." The mystery of godliness is that God in the person of Jesus Christ entered this world in which we live, paid the penalty of sin, and is making men and women godly— that is, with Godlikeness.

"God was manifest in the flesh." Certainly Paul is teaching the virgin birth of Christ, but he is also speaking of Christ's existence before His incarnation. That existence was spiritual: He was ". . . in form of God . . ." (Phil. 2:6). Hebrews speaks of Christ as ". . . being the brightness [effulgence] of his [God's] glory, and the express image of his person . . ." (Heb. 1:3). The Lord Jesus Himself said, "God is a Spirit . . ." (John 4:24).

Now from this condition as God—not seen with human eyes— Christ came into manifestation—into sight—in the flesh. He became a man and entered into human conditions. And under these human conditions the attributes of His essential spiritual personality were veiled. This is the thought John gives in his gospel: ". . . The Word was made [became] flesh." He was born flesh "and dwelt [pitched His tent here] among us . . ." (see John 1:14). Just as God was not visible in the tabernacle in the wilderness, so Jesus Christ was veiled when He tabernacled among us in human flesh. He did not appear to men what He really was; man did not recognize who He was. The One who in the beginning was God, was with God, and who made all things, became a little, helpless baby. He was the image of the invisible God and had all power in heaven and in earth, but down here He took upon Himself human flesh. Because He was not recognized by man, He was treated as an imposter, a usurper, and a blasphemer. He was hated, persecuted, and murdered. God manifest in the flesh was poor, was tempted and tried, and actually shed tears.

"Justified in the Spirit." Yet in all that, He was not justified in the flesh, but in the Spirit. He was manifest in the *flesh*—that is how the world saw Him; but He was justified or vindicated in the *Spirit* in His resurrection. There were times when His glory broke out down here; there were revelations and expressions and witnesses of who He really was. There were angels at His virgin birth. His glory was seen at His baptism, at His transfiguration, and at the time of His arrest. The things that occurred at the time of His crucifixion caused the watching centurion to say, "Truly this was the Son of God" (see Matt. 27:54). But it was when He came back from the dead that we see Him now justified. He was manifest in the flesh, but justified in the Spirit: "sown a natural body; raised a spiritual body" (see 1 Cor. 15:44). No enemy laid a hand upon Him after He was raised from the dead. He will never be dishonored again.

However, because He came down here and has now returned to the right hand of God, *we* can be justified. Down here He was delivered up for our offenses—He took our place as a sinner, and now He gives us His place up yonder and we are justified. How wonderful this is!

"Seen of angels"—it doesn't say that He saw angels; rather, they saw Him. He has gone back to heaven, and now all the created intelligences of heaven worship Him because He wrought redemption for mankind. Little man down here hasn't caught on yet, but the song that will be sung throughout eternity is the song of redemption.

"Preached unto the Gentiles [the nations]"—this is still happening today.

"Believed on in the world." Many today are trusting Him as their Savior.

"Received up into glory." Today Christ is at God's right hand. At this very moment, my friend, He is there. Have you talked to Him today? Have you told Him that you love Him, and have you thanked Him for all He has done? How wonderful He is!

CHAPTER 4

THEME: Apostasy in the churches

HOW TO RECOGNIZE THE APOSTATES

Now the Spirit speaketh expressly, that in the latter times some shall depart from the faith, giving heed to seducing spirits, and doctrines of devils [1 Tim. 4:1].

"Now" would be better translated "but." This would set in sharp contrast the early doctrinal creed given in the final verse of the preceding chapter and the apostasy within the church that Paul is now going to discuss.

"That in the latter times." Elsewhere in my writings on 1 Timothy I have said that this expression refers to the last days of the church on the earth, but I want to change my mind on that. I now feel that this refers to the days of the church beginning immediately after the life of Paul. The apostasy of the church had begun even at that time. You remember that when Paul was in Ephesus he warned them that there would come wolves in sheep's clothing who would deceive the believers. John said, "Already there are many antichrists"—already error had entered the church. The first great church was the Coptic church in Africa; it was way ahead of the others. North Africa produced some of the greatest saints in the early church, including Augustine, Tertullian, and Athanasius, but that church went off into heresy and departed from the faith.

When Paul says here, "in the latter times," he does not have the second coming of Christ in view at all. However, in 2 Timothy 3:1 where he says, "This know also, that *in the last days* perilous times shall come" (italics mine), he is using a technical expression that always refers to the last days of the church on the earth before the Lord Jesus takes it out. The "latter times" mentioned here refers to our times today—Paul was speaking of what lay just ahead for the church in his day.

"Some shall depart from the faith." Paul is warning that there will be heretical teachers who will mislead a great company of people. There will be a departure from the faith. Paul wrote also in 2 Thessalonians 2 of the apostasy to come. Actually this matter of apostasy has been in the church a long time, and it will not be new at the end of the age by any means.

It has grown and will continue to grow, however. When the church of Christ is raptured, there will be left behind a totally apostate organized church.

"Depart" is *aphistemi* in the Greek and it means "to stand away from." A departure suggests not only that you have a point to which you are going, but also a point from which you have come. Those who apostatize are ones who have professed at one time to hold to the faith, but now they have departed from it. There cannot be an apostasy in paganism because they have never professed the faith. They never professed to trust Christ as Savior. They have never heard about Him, and there can be no apostasy among them. The apostasy comes within the organized church among those who profess to the faith and then depart from it.

"Giving heed to seducing spirits." Now when they depart from the faith, what is responsible for it? What has caused them to depart? Is it because they have become better educated, more intellectual? Is it because of scientific developments and increased knowledge which reveals that the faith can no longer be held? No, Paul says, "Some shall depart from the faith, *giving heed to seducing spirits.*"

"Seducing" actually means wandering, roving, and it comes from the word *vagabond* or *deceiver* or *seducer.* In fact, Satan is all those things. They shall give heed to satanic spirits.

"Doctrines of devils [demons]." People will give heed to doctrines of demons. It is alarming to a great many people that even in our very materialistic age there is a return to the things of the spirit world and a great emphasis upon it.

Christians are told to ". . . try the spirits whether they are of God . . . ," because there have gone out into the world these seducing spirits (1 John 4:1). The test that we should apply is the creed that was given in 1 Timothy 3:16. ". . . God was manifest in the flesh, justified in the Spirit. . . ." The only way of salvation is through the death of Christ, and it is by this truth we can test the doctrines of demons today.

There is a small segment of those who claim to be believers who are placing a great emphasis on demonism. They are very interested in this subject and are reading everything they can find about it. I think that we are seeing a real manifestation of the spirit world today, but the best thing you and I can do regarding the Devil is to show him a clean pair of heels. We should not be a bunch of heels, sticking around and getting ourselves involved in all of this. Paul warns us against being seduced by the doctrines of demons. We should stay clear of them, testing each spirit by its acknowledgment of the deity of Christ and by its acknowledgment that God was manifest in the flesh and that we are justified through the redemption He wrought for us on the Cross.

Speaking lies in hypocrisy; having their conscience seared with a hot iron [1 Tim. 4:2].

"Speaking lies in hypocrisy." The apostate will pretend to be very pious and very religious. I have come to be suspicious of this pious position taken by super-duper saints who claim to have something special. My friend, if you do have the truth it will make you humble, because the first thing you will find out is how little you know. I realize that I have much more to learn about the Bible. There are those today, however, who know very little about the Word of God, but they speak as if they were authorities. "Speaking lies in hypocrisy," they pretend to be something they are not.

"Having their conscience seared with a hot iron." In 1 Timothy 1:5 we read that the things which should characterize the visible church are faith, love, and a good conscience. We should be tenderhearted people.

There is far too much talk about sex in the church today. I have heard of things happening in some churches that make my hair curl. Things are being said and done which I do not think could be done unless your conscience has been seared with a hot iron and you have gotten away from the Word of God. It is important in the plan and purpose of God that the church have a tender conscience and not stoop to such low levels.

> **Forbidding to marry, and commanding to abstain from meats, which God hath created to be received with thanksgiving of them which believe and know the truth [1 Tim. 4:3].**

Even in Christ's day there were folk who went off from Judaism into cults and "isms." This is not something new in our day; it has been going on for a long time.

"Forbidding to marry." In Christ's day there was a group down by the Dead Sea known as the Essenes. It was from among them that the Dead Sea Scrolls were found. When Christianity came along, many probably joined the Palestinian church and helped to produce most of its characteristic heresies, including the regulation of not marrying.

"Commanding to abstain from meats." There are those who make certain rules and regulations about diet that are not in the Word of God. They go off on this as if food could commend them to God. It is true that if you eat the wrong kind of food you will get a tummy ache, but it has nothing to do with your spiritual life, my friend.

> **For every creature of God is good, and nothing to be refused, if it be received with thanksgiving:**

> **For it is sanctified by the word of God and prayer [1 Tim. 4:4–5].**

The Word of God does not condemn food; it commends it. If you can return thanks for the food, that sanctifies it for your body. "If it be received with thanksgiving"—there are some foods I cannot be thankful for. There are certain foods that would really put me down physically if I ate them, and I cannot be thankful for them. Also, I am told that there is a place in San Antonio, Texas, that cans rattlesnake meat! It is a delicacy, they say. Well, if you served me rattlesnake meat for dinner and asked me to return thanks for it, I'm not sure that I could.

But if you can receive it with thanksgiving, my friend, then go ahead and eat it, whatever it might be—it's perfectly all right.

WHAT THE "GOOD MINISTER" CAN DO
IN TIMES OF APOSTASY

If thou put the brethren in remembrance of these things, thou shalt be a good minister of Jesus Christ, nourished up in the words of faith and of good doctrine, whereunto thou hast attained [1 Tim. 4:6].

"If thou put the brethren in remembrance of these things." Paul has warned Timothy of the apostasy and false teachings that were to come into the church. There will be men who profess to the faith and then come to the place where they deny it. In turn, Timothy is to warn the believers about these things.

"Thou shalt be a good minister of Jesus Christ." Every believer is a minister, but here Paul has in mind Timothy as a *teacher* of the Word of God. That is a gift that some men have and some don't. But all believers are ministers.

"Nourished up in the words of faith and of good doctrine"—this is how the believer is to grow in the Word of God. We are not to go off on tangents about diet or some other aesthetic program as if it would commend us to God. Instead our diet is to be "nourished up in the words of faith and of good doctrine."

"Whereunto thou hast attained." Some interpreters think that there was a danger in Ephesus in the midst of so much false religion and work of Satan that Timothy would go off into it all, but Paul said that Timothy had attained unto the things he has mentioned and commends him for it.

Paul has warned Timothy about apostasy and false teachings, but he will mention more things that Timothy should avoid:

But refuse profane and old wives' fables, and exercise thyself rather unto godliness [1 Tim. 4:7].

"But refuse profane and old wives' fables." As a young boy I remember there were a lot of sayings that the older people would quote to us children. I remember one dear Christian woman who had some peculiar ideas. One was that everybody should take sulphur and tartar mixed with a little honey or molasses. I was fed that because my mother listened to her. I took enough sulphur and tartar to make a small mountain! I have no idea whether it did me any good or not, but she thought it was the *only* thing I needed as a boy. Similarly, when it was discovered that I had cancer I was given over a hundred books on diet to help rid me of the cancer. I couldn't have followed one of these books without contradicting another! One said to eat plenty of grapes, the other said not to eat grapes. One would say to take honey, another to keep away from it. I decided to listen to the Great Physician and to leave my case in His hands.

"And exercise thyself rather unto godliness"—Timothy is to practice godliness in his life. Too many people emphasize the don'ts more than they do the exercise of godliness.

> **For bodily exercise profiteth little: but godliness is profitable unto all things, having promise of the life that now is, and of that which is to come [1 Tim. 4:8].**

"For bodily exercise profiteth little." There are those who believe that Paul is downgrading physical exercise. I don't understand it that way at all. Paul spent about three years in Ephesus where there was a great coliseum in which the Olympic Games were held at times. The coliseum seated 100,000 people, and foot races were often held there. Paul uses the figure of the race and compares it to the Christian life and walk in 1 Corinthians 9:24–27. I believe Paul knew something about exercise. I stood in the city of Sardis one time and observed the Roman road that was being excavated to the east and the west of that city. Paul walked that road nineteen hundred years ago, preaching the gospel of Christ. He didn't travel in a bus or in an automobile. He didn't ride a horse or even a donkey. Paul *walked* there, and it took a rugged individual to cover the ground that he covered throughout the Roman Empire. He may not have done much jogging, but he did a great deal of walking.

Paul's emphasis on godliness rather than on physical exercise is because the Ephesians were a people given over to games and athletics. We are also that kind of a nation. Many of our cities have coliseums where great spectacles are conducted, and many believers put more emphasis on athletics than they do on the things of God. There are church officers who spend more time during the summer in the ball park than they spend in prayer meetings. Paul is not saying bodily exercise is wrong. He is saying, "Let's hold things in correct perspective."

"But godliness is profitable unto all things, having promise of the life that now is, and of that which is to come." Bodily exercise will help you only in this life, because when you get a new body it won't make any difference whether you've exercised this one or not. "But godliness is profitable unto all things." Those who argue that a Christian can fall into sin and can always come back to God on easy terms are right. But, my friend, a godly life pays off not only down here, it will pay off in eternity. The Prodigal Son lost a great deal by going to the far country, and any Christian who lives a careless life rather than a godly life will find that even in eternity he will pay for it. Are you as anxious about godliness as you are about physical exercise, about athletic events? The physical ends at the end of this life, but godliness is carried over into the next.

> **This is a faithful saying and worthy of all acceptation [1 Tim. 4:9].**

Paul is emphasizing the point he has just made. In other words, he says, "Here's something you can count on." You could count on it in the first century in Ephesus, and you can count on it in Los Angeles in the twentieth century. And we can count on it in the twenty-first century, if we make it that far.

> **For therefore we both labour and suffer reproach, because we trust in the living God, who is the Saviour of all men, specially of those that believe [1 Tim. 4:10].**

"For therefore we both labour and suffer reproach." If you stand for Jesus Christ today it will cost you something. There is no question about that.

"Who is the Saviour of all men." We hear a great deal of discussion about what color of eyes Christ had. Was He blond or brunette? How tall was He? I talked to one man who was disturbed to see a picture of Christ painted as a black man. "Why not?" I said, "He's the Savior of *all* men." The color of His skin or of His hair is not the important thing. Scripture never gives us that kind of information about Him. Even the FBI doesn't know. What Scripture does say is that He is the Savior of all men. Whoever you are, He's your Savior and He's the only Savior.

"Specially of those that believe." He is the Savior of all men, but you can turn Him down if you want to. Let me illustrate this for you. They say that a plane leaves the Los Angeles International Airport every minute, and I could get on any one of them (if I had the courage!). All I need to do is get a ticket and get on the plane. It's a plane for everybody, you see, but not everybody will take it. Christ is the Savior of all men, but only those who believe will be saved (see John 3:16; 1 John 2:2).

These things command and teach.

Let no man despise thy youth; but be thou an example of the believers, in word, in conversation, in charity, in spirit, in faith, in purity [1 Tim. 4:11–12].

"Let no man despise thy youth." Paul knew that there would be those in the church who would say of Timothy, "Well, he's just a young fellow—he doesn't know yet." Maybe there were some things he didn't know, but he was not to let anyone despise his youth.

"But be thou an example of the believers." How could Timothy keep people from despising his youth? By not acting like a young fool. When I began as a young minister, even before I was ordained, I told an old, retired minister that I felt a little embarrassed and even frightened when someone with gray hair would come into the church to hear this young preacher who was still a student. He advised me, "Don't ever worry about that. Don't let anyone despise your youth, but make dead sure you are an example of the believers." The important thing is not your age, but whether you are an example.

Paul tells Timothy in what ways he is to be an example: "in word, in conversation, in charity, in spirit, in faith, in purity." There is nothing new about the "new morality" today, but believe me, the morality of the Bible is brand new to some folk! This is God's standard—six ways in which we should be an example.

> **Till I come, give attendance to reading, to exhortation, to doctrine [1 Tim. 4:13].**

The minister is to read the Scripture publicly. For what purpose? To comfort and to teach. The Word of God needs to be read, and until the church is getting people into the Word of God, it is missing its main function.

This was applicable to Timothy personally also. The minister can grow personally only by reading the Word for his exhortation and instruction. A growing minister will make a growing church. One of the greatest things ever said concerning Dwight L. Moody was said by a neighbor: "Every time Mr. Moody comes home, you can just tell how much he's grown spiritually." Are you further along spiritually today than you were this time last year? Are you growing in grace and the knowledge of Christ? The only way to do so is by reading the great truths of the Word of God.

> **Neglect not the gift that is in thee, which was given thee by prophecy, with the laying on of the hands of the presbytery [1 Tim. 4:14].**

"Neglect not the gift that is in thee." The Spirit of God gives to every believer a gift, and Timothy had a gift that he was to use.

"Which was given thee by prophecy"—evidently Paul had predicted what this young man would do.

"With the laying on of the hands of the presbytery"—the laying on of the hands of the officers of the church. The laying on of hands never communicates anything, my friend. There are those who believe that something will be transferred to the person by the laying on of hands, but the only thing that will be transferred is disease germs—that's all!

Laying on of hands indicates partnership in the ministry. I always insisted that my church officers lay their hands on every missionary we commissioned. Every minister who is ordained should have hands put on him by those who are partners with him. That is what it means, and it is quite meaningful.

Meditate upon these things; give thyself wholly to them; that thy profiting may appear to all [1 Tim. 4:15].

"Meditate upon these things"—be diligent in your study. There is no excuse for a minister not to study the Word of God, and there is no excuse for any Christian not to study the Word of God.

"Give thyself wholly to them." I will not accept a daily devotional time as a substitute for reading and studying the Word of God. It will not work to open your Bible to read a chapter at night when you have one eye closed and both feet already in bed. Nor will it work in the morning when you are half awake, or at the breakfast table when you are about to take off for work. My friend, you couldn't study geometry, higher mathematics, or science like that. The Word of God is worthy of all that you and I can give to it, and we can never give as much as it should have.

"That thy profiting may appear to all." The greatest compliment you could give your preacher would be to be able to say, "You are really improving in your preaching." That's the best thing you could say.

Take heed unto thyself, and unto the doctrine; continue in them: for in doing this thou shalt both save thyself, and them that hear thee [1 Tim. 4:16].

May I say this kindly, but I must say it: God have mercy on the minister who is not giving out the Word of God! That is a frightful sin. It would be better to be a gangster than to be a man who is supposed to give out the Word of God and fails to do so.

CHAPTER 5

THEME: Duties of officers in the churches

Both chapters 5 and 6 will deal with this very practical matter of the duties of officers in the church. This gets right down to the nitty-gritty of church life today. There is nothing romantic in this, but it is very realistic and meaningful for us.

RELATIONSHIP OF MINISTERS TO DIFFERENT GROUPS IN THE LOCAL CHURCH

Rebuke not an elder, but entreat him as a father; and the younger men as brethren [1 Tim. 5:1].

"An elder"—the first relationship discussed is Timothy's relationship to elders. There has been some difference of opinion as to whether Paul is referring to the office of elder or to an elder person, someone who was older than Timothy. In the early church the "elder" was an office, but the word used here refers to the individual. I think Paul had both aspects in mind: he is speaking of a mature child of God, and a man who occupied a certain office. Paul means both for the simple fact that an elder was an elder—an older man.

"Rebuke not an elder, but entreat [exhort] him as a father." Timothy was not to rebuke an elder publicly, but he was to entreat him privately. Timothy was a young man, and he needed to be very tactful in his relationship with these older men in the church. In other words, he was not to take the position of a know-it-all or of a dictator over these older men. He was to encourage them and have a word privately with them if he thought it was necessary.

"And the younger men as brethren." A sweet relationship should exist between Timothy and the older men and also with those of his own age.

The elder women as mothers; the younger as sisters, with all purity [1 Tim. 5:2].

"With all purity." A minister of a church should be very careful in his relationships with the opposite sex. Nothing hurts a church more or has more frequently wrecked the ministry of a church than sin in this area. When a minister must leave a church because of such a problem, the spiritual deadness in the church is very noticeable. Nothing can destroy the spiritual life of a church more than this kind of an experience. The "new morality" cannot and will not work in the church.

Paul has discussed Timothy's relationship with the men in the church—older and younger, and then the women—older and younger. He comes now to his relationship with a third group—

Honour widows that are widows indeed [1 Tim. 5:3].

"Honour" is a very interesting word, and in the Greek it is the same word from which we get our English word *honorarium*. It has in it the thought of value being attached to something. Sometimes when I speak at a church on a Sunday or for a week of special services I receive a check that says on it, "Honorarium." In other words, they have attached value to what I have done.

The early church took care of their widows, and they were very careful about it. The care of widows was the problem that arose in Acts 6. The Greeks (who were Jews from outside of Israel) felt that their widows were being neglected in favor of the others. The apostles had men appointed to handle the care of the widows so that they themselves could continue to concentrate on the preaching of the Word. Paul is giving instruction here as to how the care of the widows is to be carried out.

"Honour widows that are wido s indeed." The instruction given in the Word of God is very practica.. It uses a whole lot of common sense and is not moved by sentimentality. Christians are known to be tenderhearted, and there are a lot of people today who have their hands out to us. We need to be very careful. The early church took care of widows, but they didn't do it in some haphazard, sentimental way. The deacons were to make an investigation to see who were truly widows, where the need was, and how much need there was.

There are not many liberal or even conservative churches who are taking care of the widows in their midst. This is a much neglected area today.

Paul is going to go into this in very specific detail:

But if any widow have children or nephews, let them learn first to shew piety at home, and to requite their parents: for that is good and acceptable before God [1 Tim. 5:4].

"Nephews" here are grandchildren. The investigation should determine whether the widow in question has children. Why aren't they supporting her? Does she have grandchildren? They have a responsibility toward her. This was God's method, and I think it still is God's method.

Now she that is a widow indeed, and desolate, trusteth in God, and continueth in supplications, and prayers night and day [1 Tim. 5:5].

Now this widow is "a widow indeed"—a real widow. She is "desolate," that is, she is in need. She is a godly woman, and she prays. She not only prays for the church and the pastor, but she prays for herself and for her need. She has a right to do that. And I want to say that God uses us to help answer such prayers. He makes it clear that when we find a widow like this we are to help her. It is quite lovely when we do things God's way.

But she that liveth in pleasure is dead while she liveth [1 Tim. 5:6].

But if you go over to a widow's house and find that she is having a cocktail party, I would say that she is not the widow to help. It does not matter how prominent her son, or her sister, or her brother might be in the church, she is not to be helped.

And these things give in charge, that they may be blameless [1 Tim. 5:7].

Paul is saying, "Timothy, you make this very clear to the church in order that they might act in an honorable way in these matters."

But if any provide not for his own, and specially for those of his own house, he hath denied the faith, and is worse than an infidel [1 Tim. 5:8].

My friend, I don't know how I could make this any stronger than it's made right here: the widow is to be taken care of by her own flesh and blood. It does not matter what type of testimony a man may give at a businessmen's meeting, or what kind of a testimony a woman may give to the missionary society, if they are not taking care of their own, they have no testimony for God. They are worse than infidels. Scripture is very clear here—you might miss some things in Scripture, but you cannot miss this.

Let not a widow be taken into the number under three-score years old, having been the wife of one man [1 Tim. 5:9].

"Into the number" refers to the group of widows which were to be helped. Why did they have this age limit? Because if she was under that age she could still work and take care of herself.

Well reported of for good works; if she have brought up children, if she have lodged strangers, if she have washed the saints' feet, if she have relieved the afflicted, if she have diligently followed every good work [1 Tim. 5:10].

"Well reported of for good works." Paul is saying that it is good to consider what kind of person the widow has been in the past. Check back in her life. Don't help everyone who comes along. But if she is the kind of person he has described and she is in need, you are to help her.

I wish that the church could get back to these very basic and simple principles and get away from the sentimental and emotional appeals that we hear instead. We respond to sentimental pleas from unworthy causes which are appealing to our soft hearts and neglect those in our very midst who have real need. We overlook the wonderful widow in our own church who is lonely and seldom visited. Her children have moved away or have died, and she may have physical need. Too often the church ignores such need. But if a church took care of its widows, its testimony would not go unnoticed by the world.

I believe that these widows who are helped by the church ought to be deaconesses in the church—they should render some service to the church. For example, several years ago I called a widow in my church and asked her to visit a lady whose husband's funeral service I had just conducted. The death had left the lady without family or friends, and I asked the widow to visit her because she would understand the woman's need—she had been through it herself. They became warm friends and grew in their relationship to God because of it. A widow can and should serve in some way in the church.

> **But the younger widows refuse: for when they have begun to wax wanton against Christ, they will marry;**

> **Having damnation, because they have cast off their first faith [1 Tim. 5:11-12].**

The younger widow is likely to want to remarry—and that's all right, as I see it. But notice that there is the danger of remarrying for the wrong reasons. There is the danger that she will forget all about her faith. The church is to be very careful and test the young widows also.

> **And withall they learn to be idle, wandering about from house to house; and not only idle, but tattlers also and busybodies, speaking things which they ought not [1 Tim. 5:13].**

In other words, they carry garbage from one place to another, and the
garbage is gossip. They go about, "speaking things which they ought
not." There is the danger for the young widow, who has been relieved
of the responsibility of being a wife and homemaker (perhaps having
no children), that she will become a regular gadabout.

**I will therefore that the younger women marry, bear
children, guide the house, give none occasion to the adversary to speak reproachfully [1 Tim. 5:14].**

The woman is the homemaker.

In this whole section Paul is giving instructions about the behavior
of men and women who are in the church. He is stressing that these
relationships should be on the highest level as a testimony before the
world—that they "give none occasion to the adversary to speak reproachfully."

**For some are already turned aside after Satan [1 Tim.
5:15].**

They were not genuine believers, of course.

**If any man or woman that believeth have widows, let
them relieve them, and let not the church be charged;
that it may relieve them that are widows indeed [1 Tim.
5:16].**

Each family should support its own widows, so that the church can
concentrate on the widows who are without family and are in real
need.

**Let the elders that rule well be counted worthy of double
honour, especially they who labour in the word and
doctrine [1 Tim. 5:17].**

The early church paid their teachers, and a good teacher, I think, was
paid a little bit more.

For the scripture saith, Thou shalt not muzzle the ox that treadeth out the corn. And, The labourer is worthy of his reward [1 Tim. 5:18].

Paul is quoting here from Deuteronomy 25:4 and Luke 10:7. I have known very few preachers who I thought were money-lovers; most men are in the ministry for a different motive than that. You are not going to hurt the preacher if you give him a generous offering. Be generous also to a visiting Bible teacher if his ministry is a blessing to you.

Against an elder receive not an accusation, but before two or three witnesses [1 Tim. 5:19].

If this procedure were observed it would cut down a great deal on the gossip and misunderstanding and the strife that goes on in our churches today. Paul says that the pastor and every member of the church should refuse to let anyone whisper into his ear any gossip about the pastor or a church officer. People should be able to prove their accusations before witnesses. The important thing is that you should have the facts before you talk. And if you have the facts, rather than scatter the scandal abroad, you should seek to correct the problem by going to the proper authorities. Any accusation should be given before more than one witness.

Them that sin rebuke before all, that others also may fear [1 Tim. 5:20].

If the facts are known that a church leader *has* sinned, he is to be rebuked. The question arises, Is this to be done publicly? I believe that when a member of a church sins and it does not concern the congregation it should never be brought out into the open, nor should it be confessed publicly. However, when a leader of the church, an officer in the church, sins, and it has hurt the church, then I think it is time to call names. It may also be time to drop his name from the roll of membership. Great harm can be done to a church by sin in the life of its leaders, and this is the way Paul says it should be dealt with.

**I charge thee before God, and the Lord Jesus Christ, and
the elect angels, that thou observe these things without
preferring one before another, doing nothing by partiality [1 Tim. 5:21].**

Timothy is to treat everyone in the church alike. There may be an officer in the church who is a wealthy man and who has been good to the
pastor. Perhaps he has bought the pastor a suit of clothes or helped
him buy a new car. A pastor will often brag that such a man is a member of his church, and he may not feel inclined to bring any charges
against him even though it is evident the man is guilty. Paul says that
we are *not* to show partiality in the church. James said the same thing
in James 2.

**Lay hands suddenly on no man, neither be partaker of
other men's sins: keep thyself pure [1 Tim. 5:22].**

We read earlier that the officers were to be installed by the laying on of
hands (see 1 Tim. 4:14). We saw that the laying on of hands indicates
partnership in the ministry. The thought here is that this is not to be
done "suddenly," not to a neophyte, someone who has been recently
converted.

If we exalt a young Christian to the position of a teacher before he
is thoroughly grounded in the Word, the theology he teaches is apt to
be weird theology. The church ought to be a place of instruction where
the Word of God is taught and men and women are built up in the
faith. Instead, today we often develop what I call Alka-Seltzer Christians and Alka-Seltzer churches—it's all fizz, foam, and froth, a lot of
emotion, and a lot of talk about love, love, love. It is important that
love be displayed in a church, but it needs to be anchored in the Word
of God. Our mistake is that we often interpret some sort of experience
as being the test of spiritual maturity. We've got the cart before the
horse. The Word of God is the test, and experience can prove the truth
of it. We can be certain that an experience which contradicts the clear
teaching of the Bible is not from God at all.

There were many young converts in the Ephesus area, and they needed teaching. It was a serious business for young Timothy to select the teachers and appoint them to teach the Word of God.

"Neither be partaker of other men's sins: keep thyself pure." In other words, "Don't compromise, Timothy. Don't let someone talk you into letting a young convert teach. You will be a partner in sin if you do. Make sure the teachers are anchored in the Word of God."

> **Drink no longer water, but use a little wine for thy stomach's sake and thine often infirmities [1 Tim. 5:23].**

I have to smile when I read this verse. It has certainly been abused in its many interpretations. Obviously the wine is not being used as a beverage but as a medicine.

> **Some men's sins are open beforehand, going before to judgment; and some men they follow after [1 Tim. 5:24].**

Sometimes God will judge a Christian's sins right here and now, but if He doesn't judge him immediately it does not mean that He is not going to judge. I have observed this over many years and have seen that eventually God will move in judgment.

Paul wrote about this to the Corinthians because there were some who were not commemorating the Lord's Supper in the proper manner. He said, "For this cause many are weak and sickly among you, and many sleep" (1 Cor. 11:30). Paul said that some were already being judged by God. Some were actually sick; others had died as a judgment of God.

Paul went on in 1 Corinthians to say, "For if we would judge ourselves, we should not be judged" (1 Cor. 11:31). When a Christian sins, he can judge himself. That doesn't mean he is just to feel sorry for his sin. He is to deal with it: that is, if it has hurt somebody, he's to make it right; *and* he is to turn from that sin. If he doesn't do these things, he has not judged himself.

First Corinthians continues: "But when we are judged, we are chastened of the Lord, that we should not be condemned with the world" (1 Cor. 11:32). The world commits these sins, and God judges.

Neither is a Christian going to get by with them: either you will judge yourself, or God will judge you. If you judge yourself, the matter is settled. If not, He will judge. Sometimes that judgment will occur here and now. If not, it will be dealt with when you appear before the judgment seat of Christ.

> **Likewise also the good works of some are manifest be-forehand; and they that are otherwise cannot be hid [1 Tim. 5:25].**

The same principle applies to good works. Sometimes God blesses a believer down here for something he's done for which God can reward him. Others are going to have to wait until they are in His presence to receive their reward, which will be the case of a great many Christians.

CHAPTER 6

THEME: Duties of officers in the church (concluded)

RELATIONSHIPS OF BELIEVERS TO OTHERS

Let as many servants as are under the yoke count their own masters worthy of all honour, that the name of God and his doctrine be not blasphemed.

And they that have believing masters, let them not despise them, because they are brethren; but rather do them service, because they are faithful and beloved, partakers of the benefit. These things teach and exhort [1 Tim. 6:1–2].

"Servants"—Paul is going to deal with the relationship of capital and labor. The Christian should render a full day's work for whomever he is working. If he agrees to work until five o'clock, he should work until five o'clock. Then sometimes workers leave with their pickaxe hanging in the air—they don't finish up. The Christian is to turn in a full day's work for a full day's pay.

Now suppose a Christian has a Christian boss. That puts their relationship on a different basis; it brings it to a level above any kind of contract. I know of a manufacturing plant in Dallas, Texas, where the owners are Christians and many seminary students are employed. I have had the privilege of speaking to them in a forty-five minute chapel service they have and for which time the workers are paid. The spirit is marvelous there, and one time I commended the management for it. They replied, "Don't commend us! We find that these Christian men are better workers than anybody else. It's a two-way street. They are such wonderful employees that we don't feel that we are giving them anything. They give so much to us." What a wonderful relationship!

You see, Christianity gets out into the workshop. It gets its hands greasy. It gets its feet down in the mud sometimes—not the mud of sin, but the mud of hard work.

> **If any man teach otherwise, and consent not to whole-some words, even the words of our Lord Jesus Christ, and to the doctrine which is according to godliness;**

> **He is proud, knowing nothing, but doting about ques-tions and strifes of words, whereof cometh envy, strife, railings, evil surmisings.**

> **Perverse disputings of men of corrupt minds, and desti-tute of the truth, supposing that gain is godliness: from such withdraw thyself [1 Tim. 6:3–5].**

There are some proud men in the ministry, and they do cause trouble. Pride will always cause trouble, and it is unbecoming in a child of God. We ought to recognize that we are *sinners* saved by the grace of God. Pride is a constant danger—pride of place, pride of race, pride of face, and pride of grace. Some people are even proud that they've been saved by the grace of God! But, my friend, we Christians have plenty to be humble about. We have a very sorry and sordid background. We are sinners saved by the grace of God.

> **But godliness with contentment is great gain [1 Tim. 6:6].**

It is important that the child of God find satisfaction with his position in life.

> **For we brought nothing into this world, and it is certain we can carry nothing out [1 Tim. 6:7].**

This is a true axiom. As one of our American millionaires was dying, his heirs waited outside his room. When the doctor and lawyer finally came out, they eagerly asked, "How much did he leave?" And the lawyer said, "He left everything. He didn't take anything with him."

We come into the world empty-handed, and that is the way we leave it. This is the reason a child of God ought to be using his money for the work of God. I believe that making a will is fine, but it is often much abused. As someone has rhymed it,

> Do your givin'
> While you're livin'.
>
> Then you're knowin'
> Where it's goin'.

A child of God should make sure that he is supporting the work of God in some way.

And having food and raiment let us be therewith content.

But they that will be rich fall into temptation and a snare, and into many foolish and hurtful lusts, which drown men in destruction and perdition [1 Tim. 6:8–9].

Riches will not bring satisfaction.

For the love of money is the root of all evil: which while some coveted after, they have erred from the faith, and pierced themselves through with many sorrows [1 Tim. 6:10].

Money is not evil in itself—it is amoral. Notice it is the *love* of money that is *a* (rather than *the*) root of all evil.

But thou, O man of God, flee these things; and follow after righteousness, godliness, faith, love, patience, meekness [1 Tim. 6:11].

These are the virtues that a man of God should pursue.

Fight the good fight of faith, lay hold on eternal life, whereunto thou art also called, and hast professed a good profession before many witnesses [1 Tim. 6:12].

"Fight the good fight of faith." This fight may be outward or inward, physical or spiritual.

"Lay hold on eternal life." Let me ask you a question: If you were arrested for being a Christian and were brought into court, would there be enough evidence to convict you? This is what Paul is talking about. "Lay hold on eternal life"—make it clear by your life that you are a child of God.

I give thee charge in the sight of God, who quickeneth all things, and before Christ Jesus, who before Pontius Pilate witnessed a good confession;

That thou keep this commandment without spot, unrebukeable, until the appearing of our Lord Jesus Christ [1 Tim. 6:13–14].

"God, who quickeneth all things" means God who *gives life* to all things.

"Keep this commandment without spot, unrebukeable" means to keep the commandments Paul had given him without stain and reproach. My friend, if you are following Christ, you will act like a child of God.

Which in his times he shall shew, who is the blessed and only Potentate, the King of kings, and Lord of lords;

Who only hath immortality, dwelling in the light which no man can approach unto; whom no man hath seen, nor can see: to whom be honour and power everlasting. Amen [1 Tim. 6:15–16].

"Who only hath immortality." Jesus Christ is the only One who has been raised from the dead in a glorified body.

> **Charge them that are rich in this world, that they be not highminded, nor trust in uncertain riches, but in the living God, who giveth us richly all things to enjoy;**
>
> **That they do good, that they be rich in good works, ready to distribute, willing to communicate;**
>
> **Laying up in store for themselves a good foundation against the time to come, that they may lay hold on eternal life [1 Tim. 6:17–19].**

"Charge them that are rich." These verses are a warning to those who are rich.

"Ready to distribute" means ready to sympathize, ready to share. "Lay hold on eternal life" means the life which is life indeed.

> **O Timothy, keep that which is committed to thy trust, avoiding profane and vain babblings, and oppositions of science falsely so called:**
>
> **Which some professing have erred concerning the faith. Grace be with thee. Amen [1 Tim. 6:20–21].**

In other words, don't try to be an intellectual preacher or teacher or Christian.

"Science falsely so called" should be translated *the falsely named knowledge.* Paul is speaking of the Gnostic heresy, but this can certainly be applied to all human philosophies.

(For Bibliography to 1 Timothy, see Bibliography at the end of 2 Timothy.)

2 TIMOTHY

The Second Epistle to

TIMOTHY

INTRODUCTION

The following is an approximate calendar of events which will orient us to the position that the Second Epistle to Timothy occupied in the ministry of the apostle Paul. Paul wrote this epistle around A.D. 67.

[c. A.D. 58]—Paul was apparently arrested in Jerusalem.

[c. A.D. 61]—This is the approximate time that Paul arrived in Rome. He had spent these three years in prison, going from one trial to another before different Roman rulers.

[c. A.D. 61–63]—Paul underwent his first Roman imprisonment. We do not have this recorded in the Book of Acts, which breaks off at the very beginning of Paul's first Roman imprisonment.

[c. A.D. 64–67]—Paul was released from prison, and during this period he covered a great deal of territory. It was during this time that he wrote 1 Timothy and Titus from Macedonia.

[c. A.D. 67]—Paul was arrested again.

[c. A.D. 68]—Paul was beheaded in Rome. Before his death he wrote 2 Timothy.

The two verses that state the theme and sound the tone of this second epistle are these: "Study to shew thyself approved unto God, a workman that needeth not to be ashamed, rightly dividing the word of truth" (2 Tim. 2:15). "Preach the word; be instant in season, out of season; reprove, rebuke, exhort with all longsuffering and doctrine" (2 Tim. 4:2).

You can, I think, emphasize one word in this epistle above other words. That word is *loyalty:* (1) loyalty in suffering (ch. 1); (2) loyalty in service (ch. 2); (3) loyalty in apostasy (ch. 3—4:5); and (4) Lord loyal to His servants in desertion (ch. 4:6–22).

The deathbed statement of any individual has an importance which is not attached to other remarks. This is what lends significance to 2 Timothy. It is the final communication of Paul. It has a note of sadness which is not detected in his other epistles. Nevertheless, there is the overtone of triumph: "I have fought a good fight, I have finished my course, I have kept the faith," written by Paul as his own epitaph (2 Tim. 4:7). Also, because this was his last letter, Paul was very personal. In these four short chapters, there are approximately twenty-five references to individuals.

In this little book of 2 Timothy an ominous dark cloud is seen on the horizon. It is the coming apostasy. Today apostasy has broken like a storm, like a Texas tornado, on the world and in the church. What do we mean by *apostasy?* Webster defines apostasy as "total desertion of the principles of faith." So apostasy is not due to ignorance; it is a heresy. Apostasy is *deliberate* error. It is intentional departure from the faith. An apostate is one who knows the truths of the gospel and the doctrines of the faith, but has repudiated them.

Paul here in 2 Timothy speaks of the ultimate outcome of gospel preaching. The final fruition will not be the total conversion of mankind, nor will it usher in the Millennium. On the contrary, there will come about an apostasy which will well-nigh blot out the faith from the earth. In fact, there are two departures that will occur at the end of the age: One is the departure of the church, which we call the Rapture, translated from the Greek *harpazō,* meaning "caught up." "For the Lord himself shall descend from heaven with a shout, with the voice of the archangel, and with the trump of God: and the dead in Christ shall rise first: Then we which are alive and remain shall be caught up [or *raptured*] together with them in the clouds, to meet the Lord in the air . . ." (1 Thess. 4:16–17). When the believers are gone, the organization, the old shell of the church that's left down here, will totally depart from the faith. That is the second departure, the departure from the faith. The Lord Jesus Himself gave this startling statement concerning it: ". . . when the Son of man cometh, shall he find faith on the earth?" (Luke 18:8). As couched in the Greek language, it demands a negative answer. So the answer must be, "No, He will not find *the* faith on the earth when He returns."

This view is not in keeping with the social gospel today, which expects to transform the world by tinkering with the social system. Such vain optimists have no patience with the doleful words of 2 Timothy, and they classify me as an *intellectual obscurantist!* But, in spite of that, the cold and hard facts of history and the events of the present hour demonstrate the accurancy of Paul. We are now in the midst of an apostasy which is cut to the pattern of Paul's words in remarkable detail.

The visible church has entered the orbit of an awful apostasy. The invisible church—that is, the real body of believers—is not affected. The invisible church today is still here; and, although I wish it were a little more visible than it is, it's on its way to the epiphany of glory. It is moving toward the Rapture. That is a very comforting thought in these days in which we live.

Because of the threat of apostasy, Paul emphasizes the Word of God here more than he does in any other epistle. In fact, both Paul and Peter agree. Each of them in his "swan song" (2 Tim. and 2 Pet.) emphasizes the Word of God and the gospel.

My friend, the gospel rests upon a tremendous fact, and that fact is the total depravity of man. In other words, man is a lost sinner. A contemporary educator has put it something like this:

Where education assumes that the moral nature of man is capable of improvement, traditional Christianity assumes that the moral nature of man is corrupt and absolutely bad. Where it is assumed in education that an outside human agent may be instrumental in the moral improvement of men, in traditional Christianity it is assumed that the agent is God, and even so, the moral nature of man is not improved but exchanged for a new one.

Man is in such a state that he cannot be saved by perfect obedience—because he cannot render it. Neither can he be saved by imperfect obedience—because God will not accept it.

Therefore, the only solution is the gospel of the grace of God which reaches down and saves the sinner on the basis of the death and resurrection of Christ. Faith in Christ transforms human life. We have a showcase today all over this globe of men and women who have been transformed by the gospel of the grace of God.

Liberal preaching, instead of presenting the grace of God to sinful man, goes out in three different directions. From some liberal pulpits we hear what is really popular psychology. It majors in topics such as this: "How to Overcome" or "How to Think Creatively" or "How to Think Affirmatively or Positively." It says that we're on the way upward and onward forever! That is popular psychology, and it doesn't seem to be getting us anywhere.

A second type of liberal preaching involves ethics. It preaches a nice little sweet gospel—a sermonette preached by the preacherette to Christianettes. The message goes something like this: "Good is better than evil because it's *nicer* and gets you into less trouble." The picture of the average liberal church is that of a mild-mannered man standing before a group of mild-mannered people, urging them to be more mild-mannered! There's nothing quite as insipid as that. No wonder the Lord Jesus said to the church of Laodicea: "I know thy works, that thou art neither cold nor hot: I would thou wert cold or hot. So then because thou art lukewarm, and neither cold nor hot, I will spue thee out of my mouth" (Rev. 3:15–16). That would make anybody sick to his tummy. That's another reason I call these people Alka-Seltzer Christians. They're not only fizz, foam, and froth, but they cause you to need an Alka-Seltzer.

Then there's a third type of liberal preaching which is called the social gospel. They preach better race relations, pacifism, social justice, and the Christian social order. It is Christian socialism pure and simple.

In contrast, when the true gospel is preached and men come to Christ, they all become brothers. We don't need all this talk about better race relations. You cannot create better relationships by forcing people together. Only the gospel of the grace of God will make a man into a brother of mine. When that happens the color of a man's skin makes no difference at all.

The solution to man's problems can come only through preaching the *grace* of God. We need to recognize (as Martin Luther put it) that God creates out of nothing. Until a man is nothing, God can make nothing out of him. The grace of God through Jesus Christ is the way to transform and save mankind. That is what this epistle teaches, and that is why it is important for us to study 2 Timothy.

OUTLINE

I. Afflictions of the Gospel, Chapter 1
A. Introduction, Chapter 1:1–7
B. Not Ashamed, but a Partaker of Affliction, Chapter 1:8–11
C. Not Ashamed, but Assured, Chapter 1:12–18

II. Active in Service, Chapter 2
A. A Son, Chapter 2:1–2
B. A Good Soldier, Chapter 2:3–4
C. An Athlete, Chapter 2:5
D. A Farmer, Chapter 2:6–14
E. A Workman, Chapter 2:15–19
F. A Vessel, Chapter 2:20–23
G. A Servant, Chapter 2:24–25

III. Apostasy Coming; Authority of the Scriptures, Chapters 3:1—4:5
A. Conditions in the Last Days, Chapter 3:1–9
B. Authority of Scriptures in the Last Days, Chapter 3:10–17
C. Instructions for the Last Days, Chapter 4:1–5

IV. Allegiance to the Lord and of the Lord, Chapter 4:6–22
A. Deathbed Testimony of Paul, Chapter 4:6–8
B. Last Words, Chapter 4:9–22
"The Lord stood with me."

CHAPTER 1

INTRODUCTION

Paul, an apostle of Jesus Christ by the will of God, according to the promise of life which is in Christ Jesus [2 Tim. 1:1].

"**P**aul, an apostle of Jesus Christ by the will of God." You recall that in Paul's first epistle to Timothy he said, "by the *commandment* of God" (1 Tim. 1:1), and we saw that the commandments of God revealed the will of God, but that they were not the *total* will of God. Here he says "by the will of God, according to the *promise* of life which is in Christ Jesus." How do you accept a promise? You do it by faith. That is the only way you can obtain eternal life. He offers it to you as a gift. You accept a gift because you believe the giver. You receive eternal life by believing in the Giver. The Lord Jesus gives you eternal life when you trust Him as Savior because He paid the penalty of your sin. He today can offer you heaven on the basis of your faith and trust in Him. When you believe Him and come His way, you honor Him. Therefore "the promise of life which is *in Christ Jesus*" makes it clear that through Christ is the only way you can get eternal life, my friend.

To Timothy, my dearly beloved son: Grace, mercy, and peace, from God the Father and Christ Jesus our Lord [2 Tim. 1:2].

Paul greets Timothy as his "dearly beloved son" because Timothy was a great joy to the apostle Paul. Then he goes on to say, "Grace, mercy, and peace." As we mentioned in studying 1 Timothy, the salutation includes the word *mercy* (which is not found in the greetings of Paul's other letters). God is merciful when He does not give us what we deserve; that is, judgment and condemnation. Paul needed a great deal of mercy, and we do too. Fortunately, God is rich in mercy toward us.

"From God the Father and Christ Jesus our Lord." The emphasis here is upon the lordship of Jesus Christ.

> **I thank God, whom I serve from my forefathers with pure conscience, that without ceasing I have remembrance of thee in my prayers night and day [2 Tim. 1:3].**

Timothy was on the apostle Paul's prayer list. When I taught at a Bible institute, I always had the students find out who was on the apostle Paul's prayer list. They made the list by going through the letters of Paul and noting every time Paul said he prayed for somebody. By the way, how many preachers do you have on your prayer list? I hope you have your pastor.

> **Greatly desiring to see thee, being mindful of thy tears, that I may be filled with joy [2 Tim. 1:4].**

It is quite obvious that Paul loved Timothy, and this verse tells us that Timothy also loved Paul. The fact that Paul has been arrested, is back in prison, and even faces death really affects Timothy. Paul says, "I am mindful of your tears. And if I could only see you, that would bring joy to my heart."

> **When I call to remembrance the unfeigned faith that is in thee, which dwelt first in thy grandmother Lois, and thy mother Eunice; and I am persuaded that in thee also [2 Tim. 1:5].**

Paul came out of Judaism, but this boy Timothy, apparently, was brought up in a Christian home. Both his grandmother and his mother were Christians. I'm sure that had a lot to do with this young man turning to Christ. Timothy's father was a Greek, and it is not known whether he was in the faith.

Wherefore I put thee in remembrance that thou stir up the gift of God, which is in thee by the putting on of my hands [2 Tim. 1:6].

When Paul put his hands on Timothy, that meant that Timothy was a partner with Paul; he shared with him the gift of teaching the Word of God. I am of the opinion that Paul intended for his mantle to fall upon Timothy. This young man was close to Paul, and when Paul was in prison in Rome, he said of Timothy, ". . . I have no man like-minded . . ." (Phil. 2:20). Here was a man who could carry on the teaching and preaching of Paul, and therefore Paul made him his partner. They were together in the ministry.

Now notice that Paul admonishes Timothy to "stir up the gift of God, which is in thee." This man had a gift, and Paul urges him to stir it up. What would that indicate to you? I wonder if Paul was concerned about Timothy there in Ephesus. Ephesus housed the temple of Diana and was one of the great "sin spots" in the Roman world. Paul had spent three years in Ephesus himself, and he knew that there were many allurements and enticements in the city. I wonder if he was afraid that Timothy might be reluctant and hold back from teaching the whole counsel of God. We can see Paul's concern for this young man whom he called "my dearly beloved son."

For God hath not given us the spirit of fear; but of power, and of love, and of a sound mind [2 Tim. 1:7].

The word *fear* is better translated "cowardice." I think that many of us have misinterpreted this—I know I have in the past. I remember that when I first began to travel by air, I didn't want to, but I was forced to use that mode of travel to meet my engagements. I certainly didn't enjoy it. At first, this disturbed me a great deal. I would make a flight, and then I would rebuke myself because of my fear. I tried to fight my fear.

Well, fear is a natural thing, and it is a good thing. For example, I am afraid of a lion. If there were one loose in the street, I would find a good place to hide. It is normal and good to have a sense of fear. But many of us, for some reason, have a fear of height, which makes us fear flying. I prayed about it and wondered why God didn't remove that from me, because I read in this verse that "God hath not given us the spirit of fear."

However, Paul is speaking not of a good kind of fear, but of cowardice. Paul is saying, "God hath not given us the spirit of cowardice; but of power, and of love, and of a sound mind."

"A sound mind" means discipline. In other words, God does not intend that defeat should be the norm of Christian living. We should be disciplined Christians rather than slaves to our emotions. We are all moved by our emotions. That is why people will send money to organizations that advertise with the picture of a poor, hungry, little orphan. But Christians are not to be motivated by their emotions. Our emotions are not to master us. We are to be disciplined.

How does this apply to the question of fear? Is it wrong for me to have a fear of flying? No. It would be wrong for me to stay at home. You see, if I am a disciplined Christian, I am going to grit my teeth, go down and get that ticket, and take that trip because God has called me to an itinerant teaching ministry. Overcoming emotions means not letting your emotions stop you from doing something you should be doing. When you have a fear of flying, you discipline yourself to fly anyway. But you still live with your emotions. If you do like I do, you sit there on the plane, gritting your teeth and wondering how many more hours it will be, with every hour seeming like an eternity. If the plane starts bouncing around, I have a tendency to grab the seat in front of me. I know that the seat in front of me is not any safer than the seat I'm sitting in, but somehow I feel better when I have hold of it! Paul's admonition to Timothy is a wonderful help to me. God is telling me that I am not to be a defeated Christian; I should not let my emotions control my life.

On a tour to Bible lands I didn't want to go with the tour to Egypt, because on a previous trip I'd had a bad experience there, and I was very emotional about it. I didn't like Cairo, and I didn't want to go there. But the Lord forced me to overcome my feelings. I had planned to go ahead to Jerusalem, rest there a couple of days, and wait for the tour to reach me. But every hotel was filled, and we couldn't get a reservation. Then I thought of another way. I could stay in Athens and then just fly into Jerusalem at the same time the tour group did. But do you know what? There wasn't any hotel space in Athens, either. The only place I could go was to Cairo! The Lord made me overcome my emotions, and I'm thankful He did, because I had a delightful visit, and I learned a great deal.

NOT ASHAMED, BUT A PARTAKER OF AFFLICTION

Be not thou therefore ashamed of the testimony of our Lord, nor of me his prisoner; but be thou partaker of the afflictions of the gospel according to the power of God [2 Tim. 1:8].

I have labeled this chapter, "Afflictions of the gospel" because there is a feeling today that the Christian life is a life that ought to be very easy, nice and sweet, bright and breezy. A great many of us think that we have an indulgent heavenly Father who is just going to put us on a bed of roses, remove every stone out of our pathway, and not let anything serious happen to us. A retired lawyer sent me this statement which he found in a will. It read: "To my son I leave the pleasure of earning a living. For twenty-five years he thought the pleasure was mine. He was mistaken." And a great many Christians expect their heavenly Father to make things easy for them.

The Lord Jesus made it clear that we would have trouble. He said, ". . . In the world ye shall have tribulation [trouble]" (John 16:33). Christians will not go through the Great Tribulation, but you and I are certainly going through our own little tribulations. Samuel Rutherford made this statement: "If you were not strangers here, the hounds of the world would not bark at you." The Lord Jesus warned us that the world would not like Christians. He told His disciples, "If the world hate you, ye know that it hated me before it hated you" (John 15:18). There is something wrong if you become too popular as a Christian. I am afraid that many Christians are thinking like a little boy in Sunday School whose teacher asked, "Johnny, which of the parables do you like best?" The little fellow answered, "The one where everybody loafs and fishes." No, my friend, the Christian life is not a bed of roses. We are to be "partakers of the afflictions of the gospel according to the power of God."

> **Who hath saved us, and called us with an holy calling, not according to our works, but according to his own purpose and grace, which was given us in Christ Jesus before the world began [2 Tim. 1:9].**

"Who hath saved us, and called us with an holy calling"—not because of who we are or what we have done—"not according to our works." But—

"According to his own purpose and grace." God's wonderful purpose in the gospel was hidden in ages past but is now revealed through Paul. It had been a mystery in the Old Testament, an unrevealed secret, but is now revealed in the New Testament.

"Which was given us in Christ Jesus before the world began"—all along God had this plan for us.

> **But is now made manifest by the appearing of our Saviour Jesus Christ, who hath abolished death, and hath brought life and immortality to light through the gospel [2 Tim. 1:10].**

Now this is a verse that deserves great emphasis.

"Who hath abolished death" is literally *since He has made of none effect death.* Death means something altogether different to the child of God—Christ made it of no effect. Now, God did not eliminate death. Remember that Paul is writing this letter from prison where the sentence of death is upon him. But Paul is not talking about physical death. He means spiritual death, eternal death, which is separation from God. Christ has indeed abolished spiritual death so that no sinner need go to a place where he'll be eternally separated from God. Christ is our Mediator, the one Mediator between God and man. God is satisfied with what Christ has done for us. The question is: Are you satisfied? Or are you trying to save yourself by your own good works? Let me repeat what I have said before: Man cannot be saved by perfect obedience, because he is incapable of rendering it. He cannot be saved by imperfect obedience, because God will not accept it. There is only one solution to the dilemma, and that is the One who said, ". . . I am the way, the truth, and the life: no man cometh unto the Father, but by me" (John 14:6).

Whereunto I am appointed a preacher, and an apostle, and a teacher of the Gentiles [2 Tim. 1:11].

Paul says he's a "preacher," a herald of the Word of God. He also says that he's "an apostle, and a teacher." As an apostle he had several gifts. I personally doubt whether any man since the apostles has more than one gift. I've met preachers who thought they could sing, but my experience has been that either they couldn't sing or they couldn't preach—it was one or the other. I don't believe He will give us two or more gifts, because it is difficult enough to exercise one.

NOT ASHAMED, BUT ASSURED

For the which cause I also suffer these things: nevertheless I am not ashamed: for I know whom I have believed, and am persuaded that he is able to keep that which I have committed unto him against that day [2 Tim. 1:12].

"I am not ashamed." Although he was in prison and the sentence of death was upon him, he was not ashamed of the gospel. Paul had written to the Romans in 1:16: "For I am not ashamed of the gospel of Christ: for it is the power of God unto salvation to every one that believeth. . . ." And back in verse 8 of the first chapter of 2 Timothy, Paul urges Timothy not to be ashamed either. Sometimes Christians are very reluctant to witness. We are all tongue-tied at times, but we ought not to be.

"He is able to keep that which I have committed [entrusted] unto him." Literally, the *deposit*. This means that Paul deposited his faith in Christ until the day of judgment. Or it can mean that "God made a deposit with me." God's deposit of gifts in Paul's life made him a debtor to the entire world.

My friend, you and I are debtors. Perhaps you are saying, "I want you to know that I pay my honest debts." Well, you and I have not paid our honest debts until every person on the topside of this earth has heard the gospel.

"He is able to keep that which I have committed." It is a great comfort to know that all we are and all we have is in His hands.

> **Hold fast the form of sound words, which thou hast heard of me, in faith and love which is in Christ Jesus [2 Tim. 1:13].**

"Sound words"—the words of Scripture are inspired. I believe in the verbal plenary inspiration of the Word of God and do not think that any other viewpoint is satisfactory, and certainly it does not satisfy the demands of Scripture.

> **That good thing which was committed unto thee keep by the Holy Ghost which dwelleth in us [2 Tim. 1:14].**

It is important to see that the Christian life can be lived only in the power of the Holy Spirit. Back in verse 7, Paul talked about power, love, and a sound mind, all of which are fruits of the Holy Spirit. Paul wrote that ". . . the fruit of the Spirit is love, joy, peace, longsuffering, gentleness, goodness, faith, meekness, temperance . . ." (Gal. 5:22–23).

> **This thou knowest, that all they which are in Asia be turned away from me; of whom are Phygellus and Hermogenes [2 Tim. 1:15].**

Paul gives the actual names of those who have been unfaithful to him. Back in the first chapter of 1 Timothy Paul noted that *some* had fallen away, here it is *all*—that is, all who are now in Asia who had formerly been with him in Rome. I call your attention to this because it seems to me that apostasy is not the thing that characterizes only the last days of the church. It has occurred throughout the entire history of the church. I had a church history professor who said that the history of the church is the history of apostasy or, as he put it, the history of heresies. How true that has been.

The Lord give mercy unto the house of Onesiphorus; for he oft refreshed me, and was not ashamed of my chain:

But, when he was in Rome, he sought me out very diligently, and found me.

The Lord grant unto him that he may find mercy of the Lord in that day: and in how many things he ministered unto me at Ephesus, thou knowest very well [2 Tim. 1:16–18].

Here is a wonderful saint of God. I'd have loved to have been Onesiphorus (and I would have hated to have been Hermogenes). Onesiphorus, apparently from Ephesus, was in Rome on business. He was a busy man, but he had time to look up Paul who was in prison. How lovely! Probably Paul had led him to the Lord, and you can't despise a man who has led you to Christ.

CHAPTER 2

THEME: Active in service

The second chapter of 2 Timothy is delightful. In these verses there are seven figures of speech that are used to describe the duty and the activity of a believer, which need to be impressed upon us more and more as we approach the end time.

A SON

Thou therefore, my son, be strong in the grace that is in Christ Jesus [2 Tim. 2:1].

Paul begins with the first figure of speech, "Thou therefore, my son." Timothy was not the son of Paul in a physical way. He was his spiritual son in the sense that it was under Paul's ministry that this young man had turned to Christ. A child of God is born into God's family by means of his faith in Christ. "Being born again, not of corruptible seed, but of incorruptible, by the word of God, which liveth and abideth for ever" (1 Pet. 1:23). Timothy is in the family of God, and he is a child of God. Because of this very reason, Paul says these words to Timothy:

"Be strong in the grace that is in Christ Jesus." I love this—"be strong in grace." My friend, if you think that you can grit your teeth and go out and live the Christian life on your own, you're in for a great disappointment. If you feel that you can follow a few little rules or some clever gimmicks to make you a mature Christian, then you have fallen into a subtle trap of legalism. Paul gives no rules, and the Word of God has no rules to tell the child of God how to live the Christian life. We are saved by grace, and now we are to live by the grace of God and be strong in that grace.

Let me give you an example from my boyhood. My dad traveled a great deal in his work, and he always put down a few rules for me to follow while he was away. Some of them I obeyed. I had to cut the wood, and I didn't mind that. One time we had a place with a lot of trees on it, and I really enjoyed the exercise of cutting the trees into firewood. But my father had some other rules that I frankly didn't go for. I hate to admit this, but one of those rules was that I should attend Sunday school. The interesting thing is that he never went himself, but he always made me go. Anyway, when he was away from home, I didn't go. One time I was fishing, and he came home suddenly and found me. I had just pulled out a fish, turned around, and there stood my dad. He said, "Son, are you having any luck?" Well, my luck ran out right at that moment! I appealed to him and admitted that I had done wrong, and by grace he was good to me. He said, "I brought home a sack of candy for you and your sister to divide. I wasn't going to let you have it, but I think I will now." I really took advantage of his good nature and the fact that I was his son.

My father died when I was fourteen, but now I have a heavenly Father, and I sure do appeal to His grace. When things go wrong down here, I go to Him and appeal to Him. When I fail, I don't run from Him like I used to. I have found that when I am away from Him, the whipping He gives me hurts lots worse. I don't want to get out at the end of that switch where it really stings. I come in close to Him, and the closer I am the less it hurts. I am a son of my heavenly Father. What a marvelous figure of speech!

When I hear Christians say, "I don't do this, and I don't do that, and I am following a set of rules," I immediately recognize that they know very little about the grace of God. They are trying to live the Christian life in their own strength. Paul says, "Be strong in the grace that is in Christ Jesus."

And the things that thou hast heard of me among many witnesses, the same commit thou to faithful men, who shall be able to teach others also [2 Tim. 2:2].

Paul was greatly concerned about the future. He wondered, just as we do when we approach the end of our ministry, if other men will come along who will preach and teach the Word of God. Sometimes we develop an Elijah complex. At times when I was a pastor in Los Angeles, I cried like Elijah, "Oh, Lord, I'm the only one left!" But I found out that was not true. All over the country I've seen the Lord raise up fine young preachers who are standing for the things of God. It is a real concern to us older men that there be young men who will be faithful in teaching God's Word. So Paul was admonishing Timothy to pass along the things he had been teaching him to "faithful men, who shall be able to teach others also." And God will raise up men with gifts of teaching—this is the way He moves even today.

As sons of God we ought to be concerned about our Father's business. The Lord Jesus in His humanity as a boy said, "I must be about my Father's business." Well, I have become a son of God—not like the Lord Jesus, but I've become a son of God through faith in Christ. "But as many as received him, to them gave he power [the authority] to become the sons of God, even to them that [do no more nor less than] believe on his name" (John 1:12). Now that I am a son of God I am interested in my Father's business. By the way, are you interested in your Father's business? And the main business is getting out the Word of God. But we need to recognize that we need the grace of God to do the business of God—as well as in every facet of our lives as His children.

Perhaps you are thinking that you are disappointed with yourself. If you are, that means you must have believed in yourself. You should not have. You are to walk by the grace of God—"We walk by faith and not by sight." Or perhaps you are discouraged. If you are, that means you do not believe God's Word and way of blessing. You really thought you could do it your way, and now you are discouraged. Or you may be saying, "I hope I can do better in the future." Then you do expect to get some good out of the old nature! Oh, my friend, be strong in the grace of God.

A GOOD SOLDIER

Thou therefore endure hardness, as a good soldier of Jesus Christ.

**No man that warreth entangleth himself with the affairs
of this life; that he may please him who hath chosen him
to be a soldier [2 Tim. 2:3–4].**

The Christian is a soldier. How is the child of God a soldier? The last
chapter of Ephesians tells us that the believer is fighting a spiritual
battle and that he needs to put on the armor of God. Paul said to the
Ephesians: "For we wrestle not against flesh and blood, but against
principalities, against powers, against the rulers of the darkness of
this world, against spiritual wickedness in high places. Wherefore
take unto you the whole armour of God, that ye may be able to withstand in the evil day, and having done all, to stand" (Eph. 6:12–13).

"No man that warreth entangleth himself with the affairs of this
life." Imagine a soldier in the midst of battle going to his sergeant or
his lieutenant and saying, "Sir, I'm sorry to have to leave, but I have to
go over into the city to see about some business; and then I have a date
with a local girl, and I just won't be able to be here for the battle to-
night!" A great many Christians are trying to fight like that today!

"That he may please him who hath chosen him to be a soldier." The
believer is to establish his priorities. Here he is to endure hardness,
which means to suffer hardness, as Paul was suffering. There are
those who interpret this verse to mean that a Christian is not to get
married. Well, he is not talking about celibacy, but he is talking about
being so entangled in worldliness that one is not able to live the Christian life.

Let me give you an example. A lady called me one morning while I
was a pastor in Los Angeles. She said, "I was at church yesterday
when you asked for those who wanted to accept Christ. Well, I did
accept Christ, but I made no move to come forward for a particular
reason that I want to tell you about. My husband died recently and left
me the operation of our liquor store. I am calling you now because I
don't think I can continue operating it. If you say to get a hammer and
break every bottle, I'll do it. But tell me what I should do." What
would you have said? I'll tell you what I told her, "Don't go in there
and break bottles. You won't stop the liquor business by breaking up a

few bottles. If you could, I'd be in favor it. But that has been your only income. I would say that you should sell the store and get out of the business."

In that way we are not to entangle ourselves in the things of this life. The child of God is to recognize that he is a soldier. And we are to recognize that the Christian life is not a playground; it is a battlefield. It is a battlefield where battles are being won, and where battles are being lost also. There is a real spiritual battle going on.

AN ATHLETE

And if a man also strive for masteries, yet is he not crowned, except he strive lawfully [2 Tim. 2:5].

Here Paul is comparing the Christian to an athlete. "Strive" refers to contending in the game. He wants to win, and he is doing everything he can to be the winner. Someone has said in a very succinct manner, "The only exercise some Christians get is jumping to conclusions, running down their friends, sidestepping responsibility, and pushing their luck." That is not the kind of exercise Paul is talking about. He spoke of the Christian life as being a racecourse, and he said, "I press toward the mark for the prize of the high calling of God in Christ Jesus" (Phil. 3:14). Paul also said that he wanted to keep his body under control (see 1 Cor. 9:24–27). Paul's goal was to run the Christian race in such a way that the One who is at the end of the race—the Lord Jesus—would be able to reward him and be able to say, "Well done, thou good and faithful servant" (Matt. 25:21). A child of God is to "strive"; God intends that he *win* the race. Every child of God needs to recognize this.

He is to "strive lawfully." That is, he has to play by the rules. There is no shortcut toward living the Christian life. Forget the gimmickry today that condenses Christianity into a little course or a few rules and regulations. God gave us sixty-six books, and each one of them is very important. It takes the composite picture to give us the mind and the Word of God. We are to study the whole Bible. An athlete can't cut the corner of a racetrack. Neither can a baseball player run by second base

hing it; he has to touch all the bases to score. A child of
Jo that, too. If you're going to win, you can't take any

A FARMER

**usbandman that laboureth must be first partaker
fruits [2 Tim. 2:6].**

description of a believer is a husbandman or farmer, the
ls the field and sows the seed of the Word of God. We hear a
today about "laying sheaves at the feet of Jesus." I certainly
hope tha we will be able to put a few there, but also there has to be the
sowing and laboring in the field. After the farmer has done that, there
will be a harvest. This is the reason I don't cooperate with the great
movements abroad that are going to convert the world by evangelism.
My feeling is that the Word of God has to be sown, and I take the
position that the *total* Word has to be sown before there can be a harvest.

**Consider what I say; and the Lord give thee understand-
ing in all things.**

**Remember that Jesus Christ of the seed of David was
raised from the dead according to my gospel [2 Tim.
2:7–8].**

"Remember that Jesus Christ"—the word *that* is not in the original but
was supplied by the translators. Paul just stops to say, "Remember
Jesus Christ." Isn't that lovely! That means He's going to sit on David's
throne down here. Also, He was raised from the dead, "according to
my gospel." It is Paul's gospel because he's the one who preached this
gospel.

**Wherein I suffer trouble, as an evildoer, even unto
bonds, but the word of God is not bound.**

Therefore I endure all things for the elect's sakes, that they may also obtain the salvation which is in Christ Jesus with eternal glory [2 Tim. 2:9–10].

"Wherein I suffer trouble." You may get in a little trouble if you stand for the Word of God. Paul got into trouble "as an evil doer, even unto bonds." He was in prison for teaching the Word of God.

"But the word of God is not bound." Although Paul was in chains, he discovered that the Word of God was still going out in the Roman world. Even with a mad caesar on the throne, a dictator of dictators, who had imprisoned Paul to silence him, the Word of God was not bound. Thank God, it still is going out to the world in our day.

It is a faithful saying: For if we be dead with him, we shall also live with him [2 Tim. 2:11].

"It is a faithful saying" or better: "Faithful is the saying, for if we be dead with him, we shall also live with him."

"If we be dead with him" should be "if we *have died* with him." When did we die with Him? When He died over nineteen hundred years ago. When we come to Christ and receive Him as our Savior, His death becomes our death. We are identified with Him and are raised with Him in newness of life. This means that this very day He wants to live His life out through us by the power of the Holy Spirit.

If we suffer, we shall also reign with him: if we deny him, he also will deny us [2 Tim. 2:12].

"If we suffer, we shall also reign with him." I personally believe that not all believers are going to reign with Him. I believe that this verse narrows it down to those who have suffered for Him. I'd be embarrassed if I were put on the same par with the apostle Paul in heaven, because I haven't suffered as he did. I would be apologizing to him constantly for being placed beside him. I believe this verse is referring to a definite group of Christians who have really suffered for Christ. In the Roman world of Paul's day there were many Christians who were martyred—five million of them, according to Fox—because they refused to deny Christ.

"If we deny him, he also will deny us." This is very strong language. It reveals, however, that Paul believes that faith without works is dead (see James 2:17). You see, Paul and James never contradict each other. James is talking about the works of faith, and Paul is saying that genuine faith will produce works. Calvin put it like this: "Faith alone saves, but the faith that saves is not alone."

If we believe not, yet he abideth faithful: he cannot deny himself [2 Tim. 2:13].

God "cannot deny himself." He cannot accept as true one who is false. That's the reason He gave such a scathing denunciation of the religious rulers of His day. He called them *hypocrites* because they were pretending to be something they were not. If Christ accepted someone who was not genuine, He actually would be denying Himself because He is true. Therefore, we should be genuine, my friend.

Of these things put them in remembrance, charging them before the Lord that they strive not about words to no profit, but to the subverting of the hearers [2 Tim. 2:14].

"Strive not about words" means *disputes* of words. God's people need to stick to essentials. We don't need to argue about empty words or philosophies or our little differences. The pastor of an Assembly of God church wrote to me saying that he appreciated our ministry and that he recommends our notes and outlines to his church, although we don't agree on everything. And we don't—I can't see his point of view on some matters and he can't see mine. Perhaps when we get to heaven, we will find it true that there are three sides to every question: your side, my side, and the right side. Maybe the Lord will have to straighten out both of us. But the important thing is that he and I ought not to argue since we agree on the essentials. And that is the away we both want it. I think we waste a lot of time in a negative approach and trying to correct other believers. Instead of doing that, let's try to stay on the positive side and enjoy each other's fellowship in the gospel.

A WORKMAN, A TEACHER

Study to shew thyself approved unto God, a workman that needeth not to be ashamed, rightly dividing the word of truth [2 Tim. 2:15].

"Study to shew thyself approved unto God." You are to study, eager to do your utmost, to present yourself approved unto God. The workman here is evidently a teacher, which means he is to be a diligent student of the Word of God.

"Rightly dividing the word of truth" means to handle rightly the Word of God. To rightly divide the Word the Christian is to be a skilled workman like an artisan. The student of the Word must understand that the Word of God is one great bundle of truth and that it has certain right divisions. The Bible is built according to a certain law and structure which must be observed and obeyed as you go through the Word of God. You can't just lift out a verse here and a verse there and choose to ignore a passage here and a passage there. It is so easy to do this, but the Bible is not that kind of Book. This is the reason I maintain that the Bible is to be taught in its entirety.

Here is a quotation that reveals the ignorance of a man who failed to recognize that the Word of God is one great unity that needs to be rightly divided to be understood. I'm quoting from an article: "In short, one way to describe the Bible, written by many different hands over a period of three thousand years and more, would be to say that it is a disorderly collection of sixty-odd books which are often tedious, barbaric, obscure, and teeming with contradictions and inconsistencies. It is a swarming compost of a book, an Irish stew of poetry and propaganda, law and legalism, myth and murk, history and hysteria." That man really spoke a mouthful. His verbiage is quite verbose and reveals a woeful ignorance of the Bible. And he reveals the result of not rightly dividing the Word of God.

Now what is meant by rightly dividing the Word of truth? Well, there are certain dispensations in the Word of God, different methods whereby God dealt with man. The basis of salvation always remains the same. Man is saved only by believing in the atoning death of Christ. But man expresses his faith in God in different ways. For example, Abel and Abraham brought little lambs to sacrifice to the Lord. But I hope you don't take a lamb to church next Sunday morning, because you would be entirely out of order. It's all right for Mary to have a little lamb that follows her to school, but your little lamb should not follow you to church. The reason is that the Lamb of God that taketh away the sin of the world has already come. That Lamb is Jesus (see John 1:29). You see, Abel and Abraham looked forward to the Lamb of God, and we look back to His death. That is an illustration of rightly dividing the Word of truth. I wish that the man who wrote the article I quoted knew a little bit about the Bible. In his article he says that the Bible is the Book nobody reads, and obviously he belongs in that class. Before any person can speak authoritatively on any subject he has to know the subject. I would certainly recommend that this man study the Bible before he attempts to write about it!

A child of God needs to *study* the Word of God. When I began my study for the ministry, I attended a denominational school, and I confess that the Bible was utter confusion to me. At that point I would have agreed with the author of this article. Then there was placed in my hands a *Scofield Reference Bible*, and I sat under the teaching of a wonderful pastor who led me to listen to men like Dr. Harry Ironside, Dr. Lewis Sperry Chafer, and Dr. Arthur I. Brown. Those men blessed my soul, and the Bible became a new Book to me. It started making sense because it was being rightly divided, according to dispensations which exhibit the progressive order of God's dealings with humanity. For instance, to recognize the distinction between law and grace is basic to the understanding of the Scriptures. And Paul is telling Timothy to *study*, to be diligent in his study of the Word so that he may be a teacher who rightly divides the Word of truth.

But shun profane and vain babblings: for they will increase unto more ungodliness [2 Tim. 2:16].

Avoid empty chatter that has no value whatsoever.

> **And their word will eat as doth a canker: of whom is Hymenaeus and Philetus [2 Tim. 2:17].**

I don't know much about these two men Paul mentions here, but they apparently were apostates.

> **Who concerning the truth have erred, saying that the resurrection is past already; and overthrow the faith of some [2 Tim. 2:18].**

In that day, there were some who were teaching that the resurrection had already taken place, which meant that those still living had missed it!

> **Nevertheless the foundation of God standeth sure, having this seal, The Lord knoweth them that are his. And, Let every one that nameth the name of Christ depart from iniquity [2 Tim. 2:19].**

"Having this seal." The seal was a mark of authentication and ownership. "The Lord knoweth them that are his." Back in Deuteronomy 6:8–9, God told His people to take His commandments, "And thou shalt bind them for a sign upon thine hand, and they shall be as frontlets between thine eyes. And thou shalt write them upon the posts of thy house, and on thy gates." The Israelite was to use his house as a billboard for the Word of God. That identified him as a worshiper of God.

Now how about the believer today? How does he advertise the fact that he is a child of God? "Let every one that nameth the name of Christ depart from iniquity." That is how the people are going to know who belongs to God. This is what separation is: separation from evil and separation unto Christ. If you name the name of Christ, be sure you're not living in sin. Unfortunately, there are some who assert fundamental doctrines and faith, and then it turns out that they have had an affair with a woman or have been proven dishonest. The Lord knows those who are His because He can discern the heart, but all that the world can look at is the outward life. My friend, the world certainly makes sin look attractive by clever advertisements on billboards. How do we as believers compare? Are our lives an attractive advertisement for Christ?

A VESSEL

But in a great house there are not only vessels of gold and of silver, but also of wood and of earth; and some to honour, and some to dishonour.

If a man therefore purge himself from these, he shall be a vessel unto honour, sanctified, and meet for the master's use, and prepared unto every good work [2 Tim. 2:20–21].

In these verses a believer is pictured as a vessel. If a vessel is to be usable, it must be clean. For example, imagine you are walking across a desert, and you come to an oasis. You are parched and almost dying of thirst. You find two cups there. One is made of gold and highly ornamented, but it's dirty. The other is an old crock cup. It will just barely hold water because it is cracked, but it is clean. Which one would you use? Now give God credit for having as much intelligence as you have. He too uses clean vessels; He does not use dirty vessels. Remember in the second chapter of John's gospel we read of the Lord Jesus making wine at a wedding. He had the servants drag out the old beat-up crocks (which the Jews used for purification) and had them filled with water. He took those old unattractive crocks and used them for His glory. And today God is looking for clean vessels to use—not beautiful, but *clean.*

Flee also youthful lusts: but follow righteousness, faith, charity, peace, with them that call on the Lord out of a pure heart [2 Tim. 2:22].

Oh, how many times He has placed together "faith, love, and peace," and they do sum up the Christian life. These things should not be just mouthed from the pulpit but should be lived out through the lives of those in the pew.

But foolish and unlearned questions avoid, knowing that they do gender strifes [2 Tim. 2:23].

Some folk are continually wanting to argue with me about nonessentials. I don't have time for that. We are living in a world that is on fire! Let's get the Word of God to it before it is too late.

A SERVANT

And the servant of the Lord must not strive; but be gentle unto all men, apt to teach, patient,

In meekness instructing those that oppose themselves; if God peradventure will give them repentance to the acknowledging of the truth [2 Tim. 2:24–25].

Finally, a believer is like a servant, and he is to be gentle to all men. It may seem like we have a contradiction here. The soldier was to fight, but the servant is not to fight. Is this a contradiction? No, it is a paradox. When you are standing for the truth, you are to be definite and let people know where you stand. Don't be a coward! Someone has put it this way, "It is said that silence is golden, but sometimes it is just yellow!" My friend, *stand* for the truth. However—

"In meekness instructing those that oppose themselves." If you are trying to win a person to Christ, don't argue with him. If he disagrees with you, let him disagree with you. Just keep on giving him the Word of God.

And that they may recover themselves out of the snare of the devil, who are taken captive by him at his will [2 Tim. 2:26].

CHAPTER 3

THEME: The coming apostasy and the authority of
Scripture

In this chapter Paul warns of the apostasy that will come in the last
days. He also gives us the antidote for that apostasy, which is the
Word of God. That is why this chapter is so important and meaningful
for us today.

APOSTASY IN THE LAST DAYS

**This know also, that in the last days perilous times shall
come [2 Tim. 3:1].**

"This knows also." Paul is telling Timothy something very important that he wants him to know. He is telling him what to expect and
what is to be the future of the church—it is not a very bright future for
the organized church.

"The last days" is a technical term used in several places in the
New Testament; it speaks of the last days of the church, immediately
preceding the rapture of the church. The last days of the church are
not the same as the last days of the nation Israel, which is mentioned
repeatedly in the Old Testament. In the Old Testament the last days are
called the "end of the age" or "the time of the end," which is the Great
Tribulation period. That is quite different from the last days of the
church, which precede the rapture of the church.

The apostasy that began in the church in Paul's day will continue.
Paul warned the church at Ephesus that false leaders would enter the
church after his decease. He told them in Acts 20:29–30: "For I know
this, that after my departing shall grievous wolves enter in among
you, not sparing the flock. Also of your own selves shall men arise,
speaking perverse things, to draw away disciples after them." They
won't give out the Word of God but will fleece the congregations. Believe me, false teachers shear the sheep pretty close!

"Perilous times shall come," which means grievous or desperate times are coming. That doesn't look like the conversion of the world, does it? It doesn't appear that the church is going to bring in the Millennium or is going to convert the world. The Bible doesn't teach that it will. That is the pipe dream of a great many idealists and a great many folk who have lived with their heads ostrich-like in the sand and have never faced reality.

Instead, notice what will be coming in the last days. We have nineteen different descriptions given in the next few verses. It is an ugly brood, but we want to look at them because they present the best scriptural picture of what is happening today. We are, I believe, moving into the last days of the church. My reason for saying this is that the things mentioned in these verses have appeared today. If you look back in the history of the church, you could certainly find some of these things in evidence, but I don't think you could ever find a period in which all of them are so manifested as they are today. I believe we are now in these "perilous" days which are described in this section. I don't know how much longer it will last, but I'm sure it's going to get worse, not better.

> **For men shall be lovers of their own selves, covetous, boasters, proud, blasphemers, disobedient to parents, unthankful, unholy.**

> **Without natural affection, trucebreakers, false accusers, incontinent, fierce, despiers of those that are good,**

> **Traitors, heady, highminded, lovers of pleasures more than lovers of God [2 Tim. 3:2–4].**

There are nineteen words or phrases used to describe the last days.

1. "Lovers of their own selves"—self-lovers. This is very much in evidence in our culture today. An article by a newspaper correspondent who had covered Washington, D.C., for many years, noted that the one thing which has characterized Washington for the past twenty years is that those who are in position want the reporters to praise

them. In fact, they insist upon it. That is not confined to Washington. Hollywood is probably one of the greatest places for scratching each other's backs. One actor will publicly say something nice about another, then the other one will return the favor. You find this in every walk of life. Even schools have self-love. If a man boosts a school, then the school boosts him by giving him an honorary degree. Also, you can find this in the churches. Paul goes on to say, in chapter 4, verse 3, that congregations will follow teachers "having itching ears." These teachers want their ears scratched—they want to be complimented. To be complimented, you have to compliment. So the teachers compliment their congregations and their boards of officers. They don't tell the people that they are sinners and need a Savior; they tell them how wonderful they are. It is interesting that the love of self characterizes our contemporary society. Probably there has never been a time when it has been so common.

2. "Covetous" means lovers of money. This follows self-love, because lovers of self become lovers of money. This old nature likes to have a lot of money spent on it. Remember that Paul said in 1 Timothy 6:10, ". . . the love of money is the root of all evil. . . ." Money itself is not bad. The problems come in our attitude toward our money. Covetousness reveals itself not only in the acquisition of wealth but also in the use of it.

3. "Boasters." That word has in it the idea of swaggerers. You can sometimes tell a proud man by the way he walks. He walks like a peacock; he swaggers.

4. "Proud" means haughty.

5. "Blasphemers" is better translated *railers*. I remember the story of a fellow whose wife said to him, "Everyone in town is talking about the Smiths' quarrel. Some of them are taking her part and some are taking his part." He chimed in, "Well, I suppose a few eccentric individuals are minding their own business." Well, railers include those who are always poking their noses into somebody else's business.

6. "Disobedient to parents." Certainly this is self-evident. Oh, the thousands of boys and girls and teenagers who are in complete rebellion against their parents!

7. "Unthankful." Many people receive kindnesses from others

without even thinking of thanking them. And they accept *everything* from God without ever returning thanks to Him.

8. "Unholy" is profane. They are actually against God in their conversation and in their manner of life.

9. "Without natural affection" means having abnormal relationships. We are living in a day when homosexuality is being accepted as normal conduct. Yet in Romans 1:24 Paul clearly states, "Wherefore God also gave them up to uncleanness through the lusts of their own hearts, to dishonour their own bodies between themselves." Humanity sinks to its lowest level when it accepts homosexuality.

10. "Trucebreakers" are people who are impossible to get along with. They are irreconcilable—they won't let you get along with them. I recall seeing a little sign in a restaurant out in West Texas which read, "We can't please everybody, but we try." Well, you can't please everybody; there are folk who are impossible to please.

11. "False accusers" certainly abound today!

12. "Incontinent" means without self-control. That, again, characterizes a large segment of our contemporary society.

13. "Fierce" means savage. In our day the city streets have become asphalt jungles. Many of them are unsafe even in the daytime.

14. "Despisers of those that are good" is better translated *haters* of the good. We see evidence of that abroad!

15. "Traitors" are betrayers. There are some folk whom you don't dare trust.

16. "Heady" means reckless.

17. "Highminded" means blinded by pride or drunk with pride.

18. "Lovers of pleasures more than lovers of God." This actually characterizes mankind in our day. Never has there been a time when so much money has been spent in order to provide pleasure. Look at the athletic and entertainment events today. These are the things that are attracting millions of people. That is exactly the route Rome took when it went down. The mob was provided with grain and circuses, and then Rome fell. That same thing is happening today. I have always loved to participate in athletics, but I could never understand this type of athletics that just sits and beholds. I never thought that it was very exciting to go out to the coliseum and sit with 85,000 people to

watch twenty-two men working for $25,000 (or more) apiece. Of course I would like to be out there myself, but I am not interested in watching them as much as I would be in watching a ditchdigger because he is not as money hungry. I don't blame any man for making as much money as he can, but the point is that billions of dollars are being spent for entertainment because men are lovers of pleasure more than lovers of God.

Having a form of godliness, but denying the power thereof: from such turn away [2 Tim. 3:5].

19. "Having a form of godliness, but denying the power thereof." They go through the rituals of religion but lack life and reality.

"From such turn away" means that the believer is to avoid them. Let me ask you a question: If you are in a dead, cold, liberal church, and you are a true believer, what are you doing there when the Word of God says to avoid those things? All across this country there are wonderful pastors who are faithfully preaching the Word of God. Why aren't you supporting and standing with these fine men?

For of this sort are they which creep into houses, and lead captive silly women laden with sins, led away with divers lusts,

Ever learning, and never able to come to the knowledge of the truth [2 Tim. 3:6–7].

"Silly women" means silly women of both sexes. There are some people who have attended Bible conferences for years, but they don't know any more about the Word of God now than they did when they began. They have never matured. Their lives are not changed. Friend, if you find yourself in that category today, get down on your knees and ask God to forgive you!

Now as Jannes and Jambres withstood Moses, so do these also resist the truth: men of corrupt minds, reprobate concerning the faith [2 Tim. 3:8].

"Jannes and Jambres" apparently were the names of the two magicians called in by Pharaoh when Moses began the miracles and the plagues came upon Egypt. We would never have known the names of these magicians if Paul hadn't given them to us. Of course, that opens a great reservoir of speculation as to where Paul got those names. The simple answer is that the names were revealed to him by the Spirit of God. I don't think that the specific names add much information to the account, but it does reveal that Paul knew their names and that the magicians were real individuals who did withstand Moses. You can read about them in the seventh chapter of Exodus.

The account in Exodus reveals that Satan has power, supernatural power, and also that he is a great little imitator—he imitates the things that God does. Jannes and Jambres were able to perform miracles by the power of Satan. Moses did them by the power of God. This is, I believe, the reason reference is made to them here. We need to understand in our day that Satan can imitate the power of God. John warns us in 1 John 4:1, "Beloved, believe not every spirit, but try the spirits whether they are of God: because many false prophets are gone out into the world." Satan can imitate the power of God. In our day I'm afraid that in many places a manifestation of power is misunderstood as coming from God when it really comes from Satan.

"Men of corrupt minds, reprobate concerning the faith." Paul is saying that men on the contemporary scene, like Jannes and Jambres, have corrupt or depraved minds. "Reprobate concerning the faith" means that they have discarded the faith—rejected it totally. We have had a classic example of this within the past few years. There was a bishop of the Episcopal church out here on the West Coast, a man apparently of tremendous ability, but he and his family were delving into that which was spiritualistic, bordering on the supernatural. As nearly as I can tell, this man rejected the great truths of Scripture, and he made a trip to Palestine in an attempt to disprove some of the great truths of the Word of God. Well, rather than disproving any of them, he certainly proved some of them—and this is one of them. A very strange thing happened out there in a wilderness area for the man to die as he did. I don't propose to offer any explanation, other than he is a noteworthy example of one who once professed to believe the Word of God but became, as the Scripture says, a reprobate, a castaway. He discarded the faith.

But they shall proceed no further: for their folly shall be manifest unto all men, as theirs also was [2 Tim. 3:9].

The experience of that Episcopal bishop should be a tremendous warning to Christians. You can dabble in spiritism if you want to, but you are toying with something that is dangerous. There is a manifestation of satanic power about us in our day. It is an anomaly that our crassly materialistic age, which had rejected the supernatural altogether, is discovering the reality of the supernatural, although much of it is satanic, of course.

AUTHORITY OF SCRIPTURES IN THE LAST DAYS

But thou hast fully known my doctrine, manner of life, purpose, faith, long-suffering, charity, patience [2 Tim. 3:10].

Timothy knew Paul, knew him well. Paul's life was an open book, as every Christian's life ought to be.

Persecutions, afflictions, which came unto me at Antioch, at Iconium, at Lystra; what persecutions I endured: but out of them all the Lord delivered me [2 Tim. 3:11].

Timothy knew well Paul's suffering which he had endured in his journeys. Antioch of Pisidia, Iconium, and Lystra were all places in the Galatian country where Paul had gone on his first, second, and third missionary journeys. When Paul was at Lystra, he was stoned and left for dead—I think he *was* dead and God raised him up from the dead. Paul said that God intervened in his behalf: "But out of them all the Lord delivered me." Timothy knew of these things because he and his family were from that area.

Yea, and all that will live godly in Christ Jesus shall suffer persecution [2 Tim. 3:12].

I believe that we are beginning to move into a time in this country when it will cost you something to be a Christian. Melvin Laird, long before he was Secretary of Defense, made a statement in San Francisco at a Republican convention. I do not know the circumstances which prompted the statement, but he said, "In this world it is becoming more and more unpopular to be a Christian. Soon it may become dangerous." We are seeing the accuracy of this statement. Real Christianity and real Christians are becoming very unpopular.

I am not really moved today when the press cries that there is no freedom of press. The bleeding-heart press has played that theme for all it's worth, but have they said anything about the fact that real Christianity is stifled by the press? When was the last time you read a sympathetic article on the biblical position? The media stifles news that presents real Christianity. If a fundamental preacher gets any publicity, it will be distorted and misrepresented. Of course, if a preacher gets on the wrong side of the law he will make the front page; but if he saves a group of people from going to hell he is ignored. Friend, we are moving into an orbit when Christians may have to pay a price to stand for the faith.

But evil men and seducers shall wax worse and worse, deceiving, and being deceived [2 Tim. 3:13].

"Seducers" are sorcerers or imposters—either one. "Deceiving, and being deceived"—leading astray, then in turn led astray themselves.

Such is the picture of the last days before the rapture of the church. Now what can a child of God do in days like these?

ANTIDOTE FOR APOSTASY

But continue thou in the things which thou hast learned and hast been assured of, knowing of whom thou hast learned them;

And that from a child thou hast known the holy scriptures, which are able to make thee wise unto salvation through faith which is in Christ Jesus [2 Tim. 3:14–15].

The only antidote against a world of apostasy is the Word of God. The only resource and recourse for the child of God is the Word of God.

Paul tells Timothy to continue in the things he has learned. He had learned the Holy Scriptures because his grandmother and mother were Jewish women and had seen to it that Timothy grew up on the Word of God.

"Which are able to make thee wise unto salvation." What kind of salvation is he talking about? After all, Timothy was already saved. Well, salvation occurs in three tenses. There is the past tense: I *have been* saved from sin. The present tense is: I *am being* saved from sin. The third tense is future: I *shall be* saved from sin. Let me elaborate. In the past tense, we have been saved. Christ bore a judgment death for us. When we believe on Him, we pass from death to life, and we are no longer under condemnation—"There is therefore now no condemnation to them which are in Christ Jesus . . ." (Rom. 8:1). We are also *being saved*. He is working out a salvation in us, and we won't even have that perfected in this life. But as we look into the future we know a day is coming when ". . . it doth not yet appear what we shall be: but we know that, when he shall appear, we shall be like him . . ." (1 John 3:2). Paul is saying that the Scriptures not only give us the *modus operandi* of being saved (that is, passing from death to life and having eternal life and becoming a child of God), but save us in this present evil world—enable us to grow and give us deliverance down here. It is my contention that the constant study of the Word of God is the only help that any of us has. It is able to make us "wise unto salvation through faith which is in Christ Jesus." And I think it makes us wise in knowing how to live down here.

All scripture is given by inspiration of God, and is profitable for doctrine, for reproof, for correction, for instruction in righteousness [2 Tim. 3:16].

When Paul says "all scripture," he means *all* of it, from Genesis to Revelation. Somebody will say, "But don't you know that Revelation hadn't been written at the time 2 Timothy was written?" Yes, I know that. But the important thing to know is that Revelation became Scripture, so it is covered by this word *all.*

The word *inspiration* means "God-breathed." The writers of Scripture were not just pens that the Lord picked up and wrote with. The marvel is that God used these men's personalities, expressed things in their own thought patterns, yet got through exactly what He wanted to say. Through these men God has given us His Word. He has nothing more to say to us today. If He spoke out of heaven today, He wouldn't add anything to what He has already said.

"Is profitable for doctrine." Scripture is good "for doctrine," that is, for teaching. That's why we teach it.

It is good "for reproof," which means conviction. Studying the Bible should bring conviction to us. In fact, that is the way you can test whether the Word of God is moving in your life. If you read this Book like any other book, then the Spirit of God is not moving in your life. But if it convicts you, then you know the Holy Spirit is at work within you.

It is "for correction," that is, setting things right in your life—correction of error.

It is "for instruction," which means discipline, thinking and acting in accordance with God's will.

That the man of God may be perfect, thoroughly furnished unto all good works [2 Tim. 3:17].

"Perfect" doesn't mean that you and I will reach the kind of perfection where absolutely everything we do is right. Rather, it means we will attain full maturation. (There are a lot of baby Christians around today.) We'll be complete, full-grown people.

"Thoroughly furnished" is *thoroughly* furnished. That is, the Word of God can fit you out for life for every good work. My friend, I am against these little programs and systems that purport to bring you to Christian maturity in a few easy lessons. *All* Scripture is given by inspiration of God, and all of it is to be used in order to meet your needs.

As we come to the conclusion of chapter 3, let me remind you that Paul has talked to Timothy in a very personal way. Timothy had been *taught* the Word of God, and now he is to *declare* the Word of God. Paul has emphasized that in the days of apostasy our resource, our recourse, is to the Word of God, and it will adequately meet our need.

This is exactly what the Word of God is doing in the lives of multitudes of folk who write to me in response to my Bible-teaching radio program. We have seen that all Scripture is given by inspiration of God—it is God-breathed. It says what God wants said, and it has said *everything* He wants to say. For this reason it meets the needs of the human heart. Let me share one letter with you that bears testimony to this fact. It came from Nashville, Tennessee:

> I do not intend to make this lengthy. In my mind I have composed page after page to tell you what your teaching of the Word has meant to me and my husband. We were in the same boat, floating along without a navigator. Some day I hope to be able to tell you how *joy* has been brought into our lives at a time of many family problems and unanswerable questions, how in our middle years we know more love and hope and zest for living than in our younger years, how our Father used sorrow and you and the "Thru the Bible" ministry to be a great part in bringing this about. I want to point out three things that neither of us (reared by believing parents, and ourselves lifelong church-goers) knew until two years ago when we started tuning you in. We don't know why we didn't see for ourselves. We had teachers who tried to tell us, and we read the Bible. I think the Lord was preparing us. I'm able to see His providence now. But we knew nothing of our sin nature or of the Holy Spirit except as mentioned in the Apostles' Creed. We knew the Holy Spirit came upon Mary, and we believed this. But we didn't know that the Holy Spirit was within us. Nor did we know of the resurrected life. We were fighting the losing battle of trying to be good and had just about given up on it when we started

listening to "Thru the Bible." We then realized that indeed we did have to give up and that God would start us in the right direction through His grace manifested by Jesus Christ and the gift of the Holy Spirit.

The reason I have quoted this letter is to show you that the proof of the pudding is in the eating. God says that His Word is profitable, and this couple in Nashville has certainly proven that it is. When it gets into your life it does something that no other Book can do because it is the very Word of God.

CHAPTER 4

THEME: Instructions for the last days

It is with a note of sadness that we come to the final chapter of 2 Timothy. Paul will be giving Timothy instructions for the last days. Then we will have Paul's deathbed testimony, which probably are his last written words. We will detect his feeling of loneliness. He is in Rome, alone and incarcerated in that horrible Mamertine prison. He is cold and asks Timothy to bring his cloak. I have been down in that prison—I'd hate to be imprisoned there! He is lonely and the hours are long. He asks Timothy to bring his books, especially the parchments.

But with the sadness and loneliness we will also hear a note of victory as Paul gives his final charge to his son in the faith. As we hear him, we will be hearing from God the thing He wants us to hear. This is His final word to you and me. If you are not prepared to accept this, I don't think that He has anything more to say to you.

PAUL'S CHARGE TO TIMOTHY

I charge thee therefore before God, and the Lord Jesus Christ, who shall judge the quick and the dead at his appearing and his kingdom [2 Tim. 4:1].

This is a very solemn charge or command in the presence of God and the Lord Jesus Christ.

"Who shall judge the quick and the dead," the *living* and the dead.

"At his appearing and his kingdom." Christ's appearing and His Kingdom are not the same thing. His appearing is the epiphany, the rapture of the church. His Kingdom refers to the revelation of Christ when He returns to earth to establish His Kingdom. Twice He will do some judging. He will judge His own when He takes them out of the world. Also, He will judge those who turn to God in the Great Tribulation. All of us who are believers will come before Him for judgment at

one time or another. Our lives are going to be tested to see if we are to
receive a reward or not.

Paul is saying, "In view of the fact that you, Timothy, are going to
stand before Him to have your life judged, this is what you are to do."
These instructions to Timothy are just as pertinent in our day as at the
time they were given by the mouth of Timothy. This is what God is
saying to you and me right now.

> **Preach the word; be instant in season, out of season;
> reprove, rebuke, exhort with all longsuffering and doc-
> trine [2 Tim. 4:2].**

"Preach the word" means to proclaim the Word, to give it out, to herald it. This phrase is sort of a rallying cry, a motto that people respond
to. You remember that we had such a thing during World War II: "Remember Pearl Harbor." Back in the Spanish-American War, it was "Remember the Maine." This is our rallying cry today: "Preach the Word."

"Be instant [diligent] in season, out of season." In other words, he
means we should preach at any time. If someone wakes you up at two
o'clock in the morning you ought to be able to give out the Word of
God.

Notice that he does not say to preach *about* the Bible. A wiseacre
student in my class at seminary often came up with some good com-
ments. One day he said to the professor, "You could graduate from this
seminary and never own a Bible." Why did he say that? He said that
because we studied *about* the Bible; we did very little studying *of* the
Bible itself. Paul tells us to preach the Word, not just talk about it.

Here is another subtle point: Paul does not say to preach *from* the
Word. He does not say to lift a verse from the Bible and then weave a
sermon around it. Someone has well said that a text is a pretext that's
taken out of its context. We are not to preach *about* the Word of God or
from the Word of God, but preach the Word of God itself!

"Be instant in season, out of season." The word *instant* means
"diligent," or even better "urgent." There is a compulsion upon us. We
should be chafing at the bit, ready to give out the Word of God. "In

season, out of season" means any time of the day or night, any time of the year, under any and all circumstances.

"Reprove"—it should be given with conviction.

"Rebuke" actually means to threaten! It reminds me of a black minister, a wonderful man of God, whose pulpit I have often shared. I heard him really threaten his people. He said he didn't want any deacons who were not going to "deac." If they didn't intend to "deac" he didn't want them on the board. Not many preachers have the courage to say that!

"Exhort" means comfort. There are times when believers really need comfort.

"With all longsuffering" means that all of us who give out the Word of God need to exercise a great deal of patience.

"Doctrine" means, as we have said previously, teaching. Every minister should have a teaching ministry.

All of this is included in preaching the Word of God.

For the time will come when they will not endure sound doctrine; but after their own lusts shall they heap to themselves teachers, having itching ears [2 Tim. 4:3].

"The time will come when they will not endure sound doctrine." I wonder if our contemporary society has come to this place. Although we are startled, amazed, and overwhelmed by the number of people today who are listening to the teaching of the Word, compared to the total population, that group is a very small percentage indeed. There are very few church members who will endure sound doctrine. They don't want to hear it. What do they want?

"After their own lusts shall they heap to themselves teachers, having itching ears." Dr. Marvin R. Vincent discusses the meaning of this sentence in his *Word Studies in the New Testament,* Volume IV, pages 320–321:

[They] shall invite teachers *en masse.* In periods of unsettled faith, skepticism, and mere curious speculation in matters of religion, teachers of all kinds swarm like the flies in Egypt. The demand creates the supply. The hearers invite and shape their own preachers. If the people desire a calf to worship, a ministerial calf-maker is readily found.

That certainly is true today. Someone has said that the modern pulpit is a sounding board that is merely saying back to the people what they want to hear.

"Having itching ears." Again I quote Dr. Vincent, page 321:

Clement of Alexandria describes certain teachers as "scratching and tickling, in no human way, the ears of those who eagerly desire to be scratched. . . ." Seneca says: "Some come to *hear*, not to *learn*, just as we go to the theatre, for pleasure, to delight our ears with the speaking or the voice or the plays."

What a picture of our day! As someone has said, some people go to church to close their eyes and others to eye the clothes! In other words, they don't go to church to hear sound (lit. *healthy*) doctrine! They don't want to hear the Word of God; they want a substitute. Dr. Warren Wiersbe, former pastor of Moody Church in Chicago, has said:

They want religious entertainment from Christian performers who will tickle their ears. We have a love for novelty in the churches today: emotional movies, pageants, foot-tapping music, colored lights, etc. The man who simply opens the Bible is rejected while the shallow religious entertainer becomes a celebrity. And verse 4 indicates that itching ears soon will become deaf ears as people turn away from the truth and believe man-made fables.

That is a very excellent statement, and now let us read verse 4—

And they shall turn away their ears from the truth, and shall be turned unto fables [2 Tim. 4:4].

They want something novel, something that will entertain them.

When I first came to California, the late Dr. Arno C. Gaebelein, a great man of God who had been a very outstanding teacher, wintered out here in Pasadena, and I went to visit him. He asked me how I liked California, and I replied, "I love it here, but it's very interesting that if I teach the Book of Revelation, I can fill the church (even during midweek service), but if I begin teaching the Epistle to the Romans, I can practically empty the church. I find there are people who will run all the way across this area to find out from a speaker just how many hairs are in the horse's tail in Revelation." He then made a statement to me that I shall never forget, "Dr. McGee, you're going to find out in your own ministry that there are a great many people more interested in Antichrist than they are in Christ."

There are a lot of folk with itching ears. They like to hear about these strange, weird, unusual things. They want to be entertained, but they don't want to be given the Word of God. Many people have told me that, when they started listening to me on the radio, they not only didn't like my accent, they didn't like what I said. They accused me of stepping on their toes. But I didn't even know them—I didn't step on their toes; the Word of God did. I was just preaching the Scriptures. Then as they continued to listen, they found out that the Word of God was good for them. I'm sure there are many folk from whom I have never heard who tuned me in, then tuned me out—because they didn't want to hear the Word of God; they preferred to be entertained.

But watch thou in all things, endure afflictions, do the work of an evangelist, make full proof of thy ministry [2 Tim. 4:5].

The work of an evangelist didn't mean what it does today. In Paul's day an evangelist was a traveling teacher, a missionary. Paul was an evangelist in that sense. Now he says to Timothy, "You are to do the work of an evangelist," which is what he did do when he was with the apostle Paul.

"Endure afflictions"—he warned that Timothy would suffer hardships for preaching the Word of God in the last days.

PAUL'S DEATHBED TESTIMONY

Now we come to a great passage of Scripture. Paul has written here his own epitaph.

> **For I am now ready to be offered, and the time of my departure is at hand.**
>
> **I have fought a good fight, I have finished my course, I have kept the faith:**
>
> **Henceforth there is laid up for me a crown of righteousness, which the Lord, the righteous judge, shall give me at that day: and not to me only, but unto all them also that love his appearing [2 Tim. 4:6–8].**

"I am now ready to be offered." If you had gone into that execution room in Rome, you would have seen a bloody spectacle. Very candidly, it would have been sickening to see him put his head on the chopping block, to watch the big, burly, brutal Roman soldier lift that tremendous blade above his head, then with one fell swoop sever the head from the body and see the head drop into a basket on one side and the body fall limp and trembling on the other side. But Paul says if that's all you saw, you really didn't see very much. That happened to be an altar, and his life was being poured out as a libation, a drink offering. Paul used that figure of speech before in his letter to the Philippians, when he was arrested for the first time and thought death was before him. He wrote in Philippians 2:17, "Yea, and if I be offered [poured out as a drink offering] upon the sacrifice and service of your faith, I joy, and rejoice with you all." He wanted his life to be poured out. Now he could say at the end of his life that his life had been poured out like a drink offering.

What was the drink offering? There were no specific instructions given by God to the Israelites concerning the drink offering. However, it is mentioned again and again in Exodus and Leviticus. The wine was taken and poured over the sacrifice, which, of course, was really hot because it was on a brazen altar with fire underneath it. You know exactly what would happen. The drink offering would go up in steam. It would just evaporate and disappear. That is exactly what Paul is saying here. "I have just poured out my life as a drink offering on the sacrifice of Christ. It has been nothing for me but everything for Him." Paul's life would soon disappear, and all that could be seen was Christ. This is one of the most wonderful figures of speech he has used. So many Christians try to be remembered by having their names chiseled in stone or by having a building named in their memory. Paul was not interested in that type of thing. He says, "My life is a drink offering poured out; Christ—not Paul—is the One who is to be exalted." This is a very rich passage of Scripture. Paul's epitaph is divided into two sections. The first is retrospective, in which Paul looks back upon his earthly life—this is right before he is executed. Then the second part of the epitaph is the prospective. He looks forward to eternal life. The earthly life and the eternal life are separated by what we call death down here.

Paul sums up his life in three different ways: "I have fought a good fight." He has been a soldier, a good soldier. There had been a battle to be fought and a victory to be won. Here at the end of his life he says, "I have been a soldier of my Savior." My friend, all believers should take that position. There is a battle to be fought, and every Christian should be a defender of the Word of God and stand for the great truths of the Bible.

"I have finished my course." Life is not only a battle, life is a race. Paul was a disciplined athlete who was striving to win the prize. During the race Paul was keeping his body under subjection. He was attempting to live the Christian life in such a way that he would not be disapproved. He wrote in 1 Corinthians 9:27, "But I keep under my body, and bring it into subjection. . . ." Paul also wrote in Hebrews 12:1–2 (I consider him the author of that book): ". . . let us run with patience the race that is set before us, Looking unto Jesus the author and finisher of our faith. . . ." Now at the end of his life he could say, "I have finished my course"—he had touched all the bases; he had completed all that God had planned for Him.

"I have kept the faith." Life had been a trust from God, and he had been a good steward. He had kept the faith. He had never veered from the great truths and doctrines in the Word of God.

What tremendous statements these are!

Now let's return to his statement in verse 6: "my departure is at hand." *Departure* is from a different Greek word than the one used in 1 Thessalonians for the departure of the church at the Rapture from this earth. Paul himself was going through a different doorway. Believers who are living when the Rapture takes place will not go through the doorway of death. ". . . We shall not all sleep, but we shall all be changed, In a moment, in the twinkling of an eye . . ." (1 Cor. 15:51–52). The Greek word which Paul uses in speaking of his departure is *analusis*, an entirely different word. It is made up of two words, one of which is *luo*, which means "to untie or unloose." *Analusis* could be used to refer to untying anything, but basically it was a nautical term used for a ship which was tied up at the harbor, ready to put out to sea.

Paul had an altogether different conception than that which is popular today. I've heard this so often at funeral services: "Dear Brother So-and-So. He's come into the harbor at last. He's been out yonder on a pretty wild sea, but the voyage is over now, and he's come into the harbor." Paul is really saying just the opposite of this. He's saying, "I've been tied down to the harbor." And that is what life is—we haven't been anywhere yet; we've just been tied down to this little earth.

I know of only one writer from the past who has caught this meaning of Paul's. Tennyson wrote as the first verse of his poem, "Crossing the Bar":

> Sunset and evening star,
>   And one clear call for me!
> And may there be no moaning of the bar,
>   When I put out to sea.

That's what death is for the child of God. It is a release for us.

Paul says, "Don't look at my execution and let blood make you sick. I'm like a ship that has been tied up at the harbor. When death comes, I'm really taking off to go and be with Christ, which will be far better."

"Henceforth there is laid up for me a crown of righteousness, which the Lord, the righteous judge, shall give me at that day." This brings us to the positive side. Paul is looking forward to the future. He is expecting a crown of righteousness. A crown is a reward, and he will receive his reward someday. I don't think it has been given to him yet, but the Lord has it for him when He starts passing them out.

There are several such crowns mentioned in the New Testament. For example, 1 Corinthians 9:24–25 reads: "Know ye not that they which run in a race run all, but one receiveth the prize? So run, that ye may obtain. And every man that striveth for the mastery is temperate in all things. Now they do it to obtain a corruptible crown; but we an incorruptible." That is the athlete's crown for being a winner on the racetrack of life. Also there is the soulwinner's crown, mentioned in Philippians 4:1: ". . . my brethren dearly beloved and longed for, my joy and crown. . . ." A crown is given for having a part in leading folk to the Lord. Paul will have many crowns—there is no doubt about that.

"A crown of righteousness" is, I believe, the reward for a righteous life, and Paul will receive that.

"Unto all them also that love his appearing" does not refer to doctrine you hold regarding His appearing. You may be a premillennialist, a postmillennialist, or an amillennialist. I have news for you: there's no reward for holding any one of those views. The question is: Do you *love* His appearing? To love His appearing means that you will have to love *Him*. Oh, my friend, do you have a close relationship with Him? Have you ever told Him that you love Him? (I have a notion that Paul told the Lord every day that he loved Him, because he had hated and persecuted Him before.) There is a crown for those who love His appearing. I would like to have that crown. I believe it will shine brighter than all the others.

PAUL'S LAST WORDS

We have heard a triumphant note in the preceding verses, but now it's not so triumphant. Paul faces the reality of his situation.

Do thy diligence to come shortly unto me [2 Tim. 4:9].

Why does he say this? He is lonesome. When I visited that Mamertine prison, I thought of these words.

For Demas hath forsaken me, having loved this present world, and is departed unto Thessalonica; Crescens to Galatia, Titus unto Dalmatia [2 Tim. 4:10].

Demas took off—he couldn't stand the heat. So he left Paul and went to Thessalonica, which was quite a distance.

"Titus unto Dalmatia." I don't know if these other brethren had a legitimate excuse for leaving Paul, but I think Titus did. Paul probably sent him to Dalmatia to perform a ministry in his behalf. I don't know enough about Crescens to defend him.

Only Luke is with me. Take Mark, and bring him with thee: for he is profitable to me for the ministry [2 Tim. 4:11].

"Only Luke is with me"—good old Dr. Luke stood by Paul clear to the end.

"Take Mark, and bring him with thee." Remember that Paul wouldn't take John Mark with him on his second missionary journey. But Paul had been wrong about Mark, and now he was able to say that Mark was profitable to him in his ministry—and I am glad he said that here as one of his last words.

And Tychicus have I sent to Ephesus [2 Tim. 4:12].

Paul sent him back to Ephesus because he was the pastor of the church there. He couldn't stick around Rome indefinitely since he was pastoring a church.

Now notice something that is quite revealing—

> **The cloak that I left at Troas with Carpus, when thou comest, bring with thee, and the books, but especially the parchments [2 Tim. 4:13].**

Paul asks for his cloak or coat which he had left at Troas. This reveals a little of Paul's suffering. I have been in that prison in May and June, and it was cold in there. This is a request for his physical need.

"And the books, but especially the parchments"—he needed something to read, something for his mind.

> **Alexander the coppersmith did me much evil: the Lord reward him according to his works [2 Tim. 4:14].**

His "reward" won't be what Alexander would consider a reward! I am sure God will judge him for what he did to Paul.

> **Of whom be thou ware also; for he hath greatly withstood our words [2 Tim. 4:15].**

Paul warns Timothy to be on guard against him. He is one of those laymen who will softsoap you, then put a knife in you when you turn your back. Watch out for him.

> **At my first answer no man stood with me, but all men forsook me: I pray God that it may not be laid to their charge [2 Tim. 4:16].**

"At my first answer" was either the preliminary hearing which opened Paul's final trial, or it was his first trial in Rome three years earlier. Paul was alone at that time.

> **Notwithstanding the Lord stood with me, and strengthened me; that by me the preaching might be fully known, and that all the Gentiles might hear: and I was delivered out of the mouth of the lion [2 Tim. 4:17].**

Paul had asked Timothy for his cloak—something for his body—and his books and parchments—something for his mind; now here is something for his spirit: "The Lord stood with me." All of us, whether in or out of prison, have needs in these three areas. It is wonderful to be able to say, "The Lord is with me."

"I was delivered out of the mouth of the lion"—he was spared execution at that time.

> **And the Lord shall deliver me from every evil work, and will preserve me unto his heavenly kingdom: to whom be glory for ever and ever. Amen [2 Tim. 4:18].**

Paul knew he was going to be translated to heaven.

Paul concludes this personal letter to Timothy with references to these mutual friends—

> **Salute Prisca and Aquila, and the household of Onesiphorus.**

> **Erastus abode in Corinth: but Trophimus have I left at Miletum sick.**

> **Do thy diligence to come before winter. Eubulus greeteth thee, and Pudens, and Linus, and Claudia, and all the brethren.**

> **The Lord Jesus Christ be with thy spirit. Grace be with you. Amen [2 Tim. 4:19–22].**

Notice that he again urges Timothy to come, and to come before winter. This concludes the tremendous swan song of the apostle Paul.

BIBLIOGRAPHY

(Recommended for Further Study)

Berry, Harold J. *Studies in II Timothy*. Lincoln, Nebraska: Back to the Bible Broadcast, 1975.

Garrod, G. W. *The Epistle of St. Paul to Timothy*. Ripon, England: William Harrison, 1898. (An analysis.)

Guthrie, Donald. *Pastoral Epistles*. Grand Rapids, Michigan: Wm. B. Eerdmans Publishing Company, 1957.

Hendriksen, William. *Exposition of the Pastoral Epistles*. Grand Rapids, Michigan: Baker Book House, 1957. (Comprehensive.)

Hiebert, D. Edmond. *First Timothy*. Chicago, Illinois: Moody Press, 1957. (Fine, inexpensive survey.)

Hiebert, D. Edmond. *Second Timothy*. Chicago, Illinois: Moody Press, 1958. (Fine, inexpensive survey.)

Ironside, H. A. *Timothy, Titus, and Philemon*. Neptune, New Jersey: Loizeaux Brothers, n.d.

Kelly, William. *An Exposition of the Epistle to Timothy*. London: C. A. Hammond, 1889.

Kent, Homer A., Jr. *The Pastoral Epistles*. Chicago, Illinois: Moody Press, 1958. (Excellent.)

King, Guy H. *A Leader Led*. Fort Washington, Pennsylvania: Christian Literature Crusade, 1951. (Excellent devotional treatment of 1 Timothy.)

King, Guy H. *To My Son*. Fort Washington, Pennsylvania: Christian Literature Crusade, 1944. (Excellent devotional treatment of 2 Timothy.)

Moule, Handley C. G. The *Second Epistle of Timothy*. London: Religious Tract Society, 1906. (Devotional.)

Stock, Eugene. *Plain Talks on the Pastoral Epistles*. London: Robert Scott, 1914.

Stott, John R. W. *Guard the Gospel*. Downers Grove, Illinois: InterVarsity Press, 1973. (2 Timothy.)

Vine, W. E. *The Epistles to Timothy and Titus*. Grand Rapids, Michigan: Zondervan Publishing House, 1965. (Excellent.)

Wuest, Kenneth S. *The Pastoral Epistles in the Greek New Testament*. Grand Rapids, Michigan: Wm. B. Eerdmans Publishing Company, 1952.

TITUS

The Epistle to
TITUS

INTRODUCTION

Apparently Paul and Titus had been together in a ministry on the island of Crete (see Titus 1:5). I do not know how long they had been there. As we go through the epistle we will learn something about the people who lived on this island—Paul didn't think too much of them, by the way. Paul evidently left to go to another place and then wrote this epistle to Titus, giving him instructions about what he was to do as a young preacher while remaining in Crete. The date he wrote it was around A.D. 64–67.

The fact that Paul's and Titus' ministry on Crete is not mentioned in Acts reveals that the Book of Acts does not contain all the record of the early church. Actually, it is a very small record, and only the ministries of two of the apostles are emphasized: Peter in the first part of the book and Paul in the second part. We do not have a complete record of even these two men's ministries.

In the two epistles to the Thessalonians Paul's great emphasis is on the coming of Christ—it is a bright and beautiful hope for him. Critics of Paul will point out that this was his position early in his ministry but that later on he did not emphasize it. However, Titus was written about the same time as 1 Timothy, right at the end of the ministry of the apostle Paul. In Titus 2:13 Paul writes: "Looking for that blessed hope, and the glorious appearing of the great God and our Saviour Jesus Christ." My friend, Paul had not lost the blessed hope of the church. I think it was shining bright and will shine even brighter ". . . until the day dawn, and the day star arise in your hearts" (2 Pet. 1:19).

Timothy and Titus were two young preachers whom Paul had the privilege of leading to the Lord. Paul calls both of them his sons, his genuine sons; that is, he led both of them to a saving knowledge of Christ.

Paul wrote letters to both of these brethren; we have two epistles to Timothy and one epistle to Titus. These letters are called *Pastoral Epistles* because in them Paul gives instruction to these young preachers concerning the local church. These letters also prove very profitable to us today. We have so much other instruction relative to the local church—I suppose we could fill a whole library with the books that have been written on how to run the local church. In Scripture we have only these three epistles, and they are very brief; yet they do give us the essential *modus operandi* for the church. What they do impress upon us is that if there is a lack or a need in a church, it isn't a problem with the organization or with the system that is being used. Rather, if there is a need in a church, it is a *spiritual* need.

Frankly, we know very little about either of these young preachers, Timothy and Titus. Titus, however, seems to have been a stronger man, both physically and spiritually. Paul expressed less concern for Titus' welfare than he did for Timothy's. Titus was probably more mature, and he possessed a virile personality.

Timothy was a Jew who was circumcised by Paul, but Titus was a Gentile, and Paul refused to circumcise him. We read in Galatians that Paul took Titus with him to Jerusalem, and since he was a Gentile, Paul would not permit him to be circumcised (see Gal. 2:1–3). But when he took Timothy with him, Paul had him circumcised (see Acts 16:1–3). Paul circumcised one young preacher and refused to circumcise the other. If you must draw a rule from that, it can only be this: "For in Christ Jesus neither circumcision availeth any thing, nor uncircumcision, but a new creature" (Gal. 6:15).

Paul said that he wanted to be all things to all men that he might win some to Christ—to the Jew he wanted to be a Jew, and to the Gentile he wanted to be as a Gentile. He had Timothy circumcised because they were going to go into the synagogues. But in that great council of the church in Jerusalem, the gospel was at stake, and Paul would not permit one bit of legalism to slip in (see Acts 15); therefore he refused to let Titus be circumcised.

It is a dangerous thing to put down a series of little rules that are nothing in the world but a ritual whereby you attempt to live the Christian life. My friend, unless you have a personal relationship with Jesus Christ all else comes absolutely to nought.

In this epistle to Titus we have a fine picture of the New Testament church in its full-orbed realization in the community as an organization. I hear many folk today who say they are members of "a New Testament church." I would like to ask them if they have had anybody drop dead in their church recently. I am sure that they would exclaim that they had not had that experience! Well, in the early church, the New Testament church, we read of Ananias and Sapphira who dropped dead in the church because they had lied to the Holy Spirit (see Acts 5). I think that if this principle were operating in our churches today, the average church would need to be turned into a hospital or even a mortuary!

The ideal church, according to this epistle, (1) has an orderly organization, (2) is sound in doctrine, and (3) is pure in life, ready to every good work. This is the picture of the New Testament church that this epistle to Titus presents to us. In Timothy the emphasis was upon the need for *sound teaching* in the church. In Titus the emphasis is put upon the importance of *God's order* for the conduct of the churches. In fact, Titus 1:5 is the key to the entire epistle: "For this cause left I thee in Crete, that thou shouldest set in order the things that are wanting, and ordain elders in every city, as I had appointed thee." Titus was to set things in order in the churches in Crete.

In chapter 1 Paul says that the church is to be an orderly organization (see Titus 1:5). In chapter 2 he emphasizes that the church is to teach and preach the Word of God: "But speak thou the things which become sound doctrine" (Titus 2:1). He says that the church must be doctrinally sound in the faith. And then in chapter 3 we see that the church is to perform good works: "Put them in mind to be subject to principalities and powers, to obey magistrates, to be ready to every good work" (Titus 3:1). In other words, the churc' is saved by *grace*, is to live by *grace*, and is to demonstrate her faith to the world by her *good works*.

I would say that it would be very difficult today to find a church that is using all three of these prongs, that is stressing all three of these tremendous emphases. Some will emphasize one, while others emphasize another. Let's look at each one a little more closely:

First of all, the church is to be an orderly church. Everything, Paul wrote to the Corinthians, should be done decently and in order (see 1 Cor. 14:40). Sometimes you don't find much order in a church, and often the reason is that there are a few officers who are trying to run the whole thing. Such a church is in real trouble and is a heartbreak to its pastor. The church is to be an orderly church, not run by a couple of deacons.

Secondly, in many churches you will find that there is no emphasis at all upon sound doctrine. Because of this, I always stress to young pastors that they should not focus on building a church or building an empire of any kind. I tell them just to teach and give out the Word of God. Rather than build an organization—that is, a lot of buildings—they should build into the lives of men and women. Whatever organization they have built on a church may be wrecked by others later on after they have left. That will be a real heartbreak to a pastor unless he has before him the goal of building into the lives of men and women. That should be the emphasis in any church.

Finally, a church should be ready for every good work. Sometimes we fundamentalists put such a great emphasis on doctrine (although I don't think we overemphasize it) that we *do* underemphasize good works. A church should be engaged in good works. Many Christian organizations are so concerned with getting in the finances to carry on their program that they become more interested in getting people to give than in helping those people. A lot of folk need help—not just spiritual help but also physical help. We need to *do* things for people, to help then with their physical needs.

I am happy that I can say there are many churches which are carrying on a work of helping people. I know of one church which has people who go out and visit shut-ins; they read to them, sew for them, and do many other helpful chores. That's a lovely thing to do. Our government is able to provide some care for the poor and needy, and that is wonderful, but *we* can go and sit down and talk with lonely people like this, which is a much-needed ministry today.

This is only a brief resumé of this epistle to Titus. Liberalism has attempted to emphasize the third chapter which deals with good works, forgetting the two chapters on order and doctrine which precede it. Until a church has all three of these aspects that Paul has outlined, it has no claim to be called "a New Testament church."

OUTLINE

I. **The Church Is an Organization, Chapter 1**
   A. Introduction, Chapter 1:1–4
   B. An Orderly Church Must Have Ordained Elders Who Meet Prescribed Requirements, Chapter 1:5–9
   C. The Bad Reputation of the Cretans, Chapter 1:10–16

II. **The Church Is to Teach and Preach the Word of God, Chapter 2**
   A. The Church Must Teach Sound Doctrine, Chapter 2:1–10
   B. The Church Must Preach the Grace of God, Chapter 2:11–15

III. **The Church Is to Perform Good Works, Chapter 3**
   A. Good Works Are an Evidence of Salvation, Chapter 3:1–7 (*The Works of the Holy Spirit*)
   B. Good Works Are Profitable for the Present and Future, Chapter 3:8–15

CHAPTER 1

INTRODUCTION

The introduction to Titus is characteristic of those in the Pastoral Epistles, but it is not characteristic of Paul's other epistles.

Paul, a servant of God, and an apostle of Jesus Christ, according to the faith of God's elect, and the acknowledging of the truth which is after godliness [Titus 1:1].

"A servant of God"—the word *servant* here actually means "bond slave." Paul says that he is a bond slave of God. We know from the Old Testament that a bond slave was one who chose to remain a slave of his master for life.

"An apostle of Jesus Christ." Paul is defending his apostleship. The reason that he asserts his apostleship here is that he is going to give instructions to the organized church. These instructions come from an apostle, the appointed writer of the Lord Jesus who was now communicating with His church through His apostles. The Epistle to Titus is a communication from the Lord Jesus to us also.

"According to the faith of God's elect." Paul does not say "*for* the faith," but "*according to* the faith"—in other words, according to the norm or standard of faith which is set for God's elect today. Whether you are saved or not *does* rest on what you believe. Tell me what you think of Jesus Christ; tell me what you believe about His death on the Cross and what it means to you; tell me what you believe about His resurrection and what it means to you; tell me whether you believe the Bible to be the Word of God. With this information I think I can deduce whether you are a child of God or not. This is the norm, you see: "According to the faith of God's elect."

"God's elect"—this is the way Paul speaks of saved people. He is not discussing the doctrine of election at all.

"And the acknowledging of the truth which is after godliness." This could be better translated "the *knowledge* of the truth which is *according to* godliness." The Greek preposition is *kata,* meaning "according to." My friend, if the truth that you have does not lead to a godly life, there is something radically wrong with your faith.

I was told once of a preacher who drinks, cusses, and runs with the country club crowd. On Sunday he preaches the gospel, and people come forward every week. Another pastor in that community asked me, "Dr. McGee, how is it that that man is prospering?" I told him I honestly did not think the man was prospering. Maybe he is bringing a lot of numbers into the church, but he is not building the church of the Lord Jesus Christ. Truth will lead to godliness, and if it doesn't lead to godliness, it is not truth, my friend.

Paul will dwell on this theme that when the gospel is believed it will lead to godliness because the people on the island of Crete were abusing the grace of God. They said that if they had been saved by grace they were free to live in sin if they wanted to. Paul answers that right here in this first verse by saying that when the truth of God is believed it will lead to godliness. Grace saves us, but it also lays down certain disciplines for our lives and calls us to live on a high plane. You cannot use the doctrine of the grace of God to excuse sin. If you think that you can be saved by grace and live in sin—may I say this kindly, but I must say it—you are not saved by grace; you are not saved at all. Salvation by grace leads to a godly life.

In hope of eternal life, which God, that cannot lie, promised before the world began [Titus 1:2].

"In hope of eternal life." The idea here is *resting* upon the hope of eternal life. In Titus we will see that Paul speaks of grace in three time zones. In Titus 2:11–13 we see all three: "For the grace of God that bringeth salvation"—that is *past;* "teaching us"—that is *present;* and "looking for that blessed hope"—that is *future.* This is the hope that Paul is speaking of, and he says we are to rest upon that hope.

"Which God, that cannot lie." This hope was promised by a God who cannot lie. In Romans 3:4 Paul wrote: "God forbid: yea, let God be true, but every man a liar. . . ."

Sometimes we believers almost make God out a liar by the lives we live. We say we believe something, but we don't really believe, and we *act* as if we don't believe. Paul says God cannot lie.

I have often wanted to preach a sermon on things that God cannot do. This is one: God cannot lie. Do you also know that you see something every day that God has never seen? You have seen your equal; God has never seen His equal. Why cannot God lie when we can? Well, you can do something God cannot do. You see, God *must* be true to Himself. He is holy and He is righteous—that is His nature, and there are certain things He cannot do because of His nature. It is not because it is impossible for Him to do it; but because God is true to His nature, He cannot do it. He is righteous, He is just, and He never deceives. He is One you can depend upon.

"Promised before the world began"—this promise was made back in eternity.

But hath in due times manifested his word through preaching, which is committed unto me according to the commandment of God our Saviour [Titus 1:3].

"In due times" means in His own seasons. God moves in a very orderly manner in what He does. God has made the peach tree to bud in the spring—it will not stick out those beautiful buds when the first snow falls; it waits until spring.

"Hath in due times manifested his word through preaching." The word that is translated here as "preaching" comes from the Greek word *kerux*, which means "a herald" or "trumpet." A trumpet was used in that day to make a proclamation. If a ruler had a proclamation to make, a trumpeter came out and blew a trumpet, and then the proclamation was made. That is the idea here. Paul is saying that God has in the correct seasons manifested His Word through a proclamation. He then adds that it has been committed to him to proclaim the Word "according to the commandment of God our Saviour."

To Titus, mine own son after the common faith: Grace, mercy, and peace, from God the Father and the Lord Jesus Christ our Saviour [Titus 1:4].

"To Titus, mine own son" or my *genuine* son. Paul had led Titus to a saving knowledge of the Lord Jesus Christ. Titus was Paul's spiritual son.

"After the common faith"—the common faith is the faith that is shared by all, the faith that all believers must have. It is a living faith in the Lord Jesus Christ.

"Grace, mercy, and peace, from God the Father and the Lord Jesus Christ our Saviour." The grace of God has appeared, and, therefore, God extends mercy to us today. I don't know about you, but I use up a whole lot of the mercy of God. I am grateful that He is good to me and does not deal with me according to my orneriness and disobedience. He has simply been good to me. Grace, mercy, and peace—peace is the present possession of the believer, but there is a peace coming when the Prince of Peace comes also. All these are "from God the Father and the Lord Jesus Christ our Saviour."

AN ORDERLY CHURCH MUST HAVE ORDAINED ELDERS WHO MEET THE PRESCRIBED REQUIREMENTS

That is a pretty long title, but it belongs to a very important section of Scripture.

For this cause left I thee in Crete, that thou shouldest set in order the things that are wanting, and ordain elders in every city, as I had appointed thee [Titus 1:5].

Paul had left Titus in Crete to organize local churches with elders as spiritual leaders. The island of Crete is one of the largest islands in the Mediterranean Sea. There was a great deal of mythology and tradition connected with this island as there generally was with all of the Greek islands. According to their tradition, Minos was the one who first gave laws to the Cretans. He conquered the Aegean pirates who were there, and he established a navy. After the Trojan War, the principal cities of the island formed themselves into several republics, mostly independent. Crete was annexed to the Roman Empire about 67 B.C. These chief cities were Knossos, Cydonia, and Gortyna, and apparently there were churches now in all these places. Paul seems to have done a very effective missionary work on the island, but we have no record of it in Scripture whatsoever. There is actually no absolute proof that before his voyage to Rome he ever went to the island of Crete. But from the information we are given in this little epistle, we are led to believe that he was there and left Titus to organize the churches which were founded by him and Titus.

Crete was evidently a pretty bad place, and the people were not very good people. Paul himself says that they were liars, and that is certainly the thing for which they were noted in that day. There was a Greek word, *kretizein,* which means to speak like a Cretan and was synonymous with being a liar. One of their own poets wrote, "Crete, which a hundred cities doth maintain, cannot deny this, though to lying given."

Although they were known as liars, and Paul will have other uncomplimentary things to say about them, many of them turned to the Lord, and Paul writes to Titus to organize their churches.

"Set in order the things that are wanting, and ordain elders in every city." The gift of an elder is a gift of men to the church. Putting your hand on the head of some men and going through a little ritual will not make them elders. But I believe it is important to do that with men who do have the gift of elders. I think the churches in Crete had elders, but they had never been ordained, or set aside. They were men who had a gift of supervision of the churches and were exercising that gift without an authority. Titus is to "ordain elders"—appoint them, set them aside—"in every city."

"As I had appointed thee." Paul says, "I have appointed you, Titus, and you are to appoint elders in these cities."

A man who holds an office of elder should have the gift of an elder. There are certain men who are made officers in the church who have no gift for it at all. That is half of our problem in many churches today, and the other half is that there are good men who have the gift and are not made officers in the church. As a result, some of our churches get into the hands of the wrong folk, and all sorts of problems arise.

Now here are the requirements for the men who are to hold this office:

If any be blameless, the husband of one wife, having faithful children not accused of riot or unruly [Titus 1:6].

"If any be blameless"—that does not mean he must be perfect, without sin. It does mean that any accusation that is brought against him must not be found to be true. His life must be above reproach.

When someone can point a finger at an officer of the church and accurately accuse him of dishonesty, then the cause of Christ is hurt. It does not matter how naturally gifted a man may be, if someone can say that his speech does not reflect a dedication to Christ, then the cause of Christ is hurt, and that man should not be an officer of the church.

"The husband of one wife, having faithful children." The idea here of "faithful children" means *believing* children. If a man cannot lead his own children to the Lord, he ought not to be an officer in the church. Please do not misunderstand me. I recognize that today in many wonderful Christian homes there is a son or daughter who is away from the Lord and who gives no evidence of godly upbringing. A man may be a fine, godly man who has a wonderful Christian home, and he may not be guilty of anything that caused that boy or girl to turn from Christ, but he should not be an officer in the church. As an officer in the church, he might be called upon to make a judgment about someone else. That person in turn could point his finger and say, "What about you? What about your son, your daughter? What right have you to talk to me?" For the cause of Christ and for the sake of the office, an officer in the church must have believing, obedient children.

"Not accused of riot or unruly." "Of riot" could be translated *of profligacy*. They are not to be out in a protest movement carrying placards, but instead they should be concerned with living a life glorifying to the Lord Jesus and with getting out His Word.

> **For a bishop must be blameless, as the steward of God; not selfwilled, not soon angry, not given to wine, no striker, not given to filthy lucre [Titus 1:7].**

This is so practical! A bishop (or elder) must not be "selfwilled" for he is a steward of God as well as a representative of the people. He is in the church to find and do God's will.

"Not soon angry" means not touchy.

"Not given to filthy lucre," that is, not covetous.

These are to be the characteristics of "a bishop." As we have said before, elder and bishop are synonymous terms. The word *elder (presbuteros)* refers to the individual, and he was to be a mature person both physically and spiritually. A *bishop (episkopos)* was an overseer; he ruled the church. Therefore, this word has reference to the office. But never was a church to have only one man made bishop or presbyter. There were always several.

There has been some disagreement as to whether there were elders already in the churches in Crete and Titus was to ordain them, or whether there were none and Titus was to now appoint some. If the latter was the case (which I do not think it was), then I feel that the churches would have had to agree upon the men Titus appointed. However, that is not the main issue, and it should not be the issue in churches today. Paul's emphasis is upon a man's personal requirements to hold such a position in a church.

> **But a lover of hospitality, a lover of good men, sober, just, holy, temperate [Titus 1:8].**

These are the requirements of the elder, and their meaning is familiar to us.

> **Holding fast the faithful word as he hath been taught, that he may be able by sound doctrine both to exhort and to convince the gainsayers [Titus 1:9].**

A better rendering of this verse would be: "Holding fast the trustworthy word according to the teaching, that he may be able to exhort in the sound teaching and to convict the gainsayers (heretics)."

There were two things that an officer should be able to do: (1) He should be able to exhort, that is, to teach the Word of God; and (2) he must be able to confute or refute the heretics. I feel that men who hold office in a church should be Bible-trained men. During World War II we had what was called "ninety-day wonders." The army needed more officers and so they put them through a short course in a hurry, and they came up with some rather peculiar second lieutenants in those days. Remember that Paul told Timothy to "lay hands suddenly on no man . . ." (1 Tim. 5:22). You are not to have a man converted one night, ask him to give his testimony the next night, make him an officer in the church on the third night, an evangelist on the fourth, and the pastor of the church on the fifth night! We sometimes do things like that today, and it is very unfortunate for the church. A church officer should be able to stand on the Word of God and to give it out.

THE BAD REPUTATION OF THE CRETANS

Paul is now going to talk about the bad reputation of the Cretans. We must remember that all men are sinners; we are all brothers in the sense that we are all sinners. All men are not in the brotherhood of God, because that comes only through the New Birth by becoming a son of God through faith in Christ. But surely we are all sons of Adam, and "in Adam all die," because all have sinned (see 1 Cor. 15:22). However, these Cretans had a particularly bad reputation:

For there are many unruly and vain talkers and deceivers, specially they of the circumcision [Titus 1:10].

"Vain talkers" means empty chatterers. There are certain Christians (perhaps you know some) who are rather frothy at the mouth; they just talk a blue streak. I rode once with a man for two hundred miles, and from the moment I got in his car until I got out, the only thing I had to do was grunt and he would keep on talking! If you had added up all he had to say, it was just a great big bag of nothing, a whole lot of hot air. There are many empty talkers. It is all right to have fun and be light-hearted, but what Paul is condemning is constant chattering with nothing but empty words.

"Deceivers, specially they of the circumcision." Paul is referring to those who were seeking to contradict his teaching.

Whose mouths must be stopped, who subvert whole houses, teaching things which they ought not, for filthy lucre's sake [Titus 1:11].

"Who subvert whole houses" means to overthrow whole families. This was very serious. Wherever the Word of God is sown, the Devil gets in—he's the enemy and he always sows tares among the wheat. I have found this to be true in my own experience. I was back East one time in an area in which our radio program is heard. We are reaching multitudes there, and many have come to Christ. But while I was there I learned that our broadcast is immediately followed by the broadcast of one of the cults. The speaker on that program attempts to "correct" my teaching of the Bible—the Devil always gets in. Similarly, a great work of Christ had been done in Crete, but the enemy was right there to sow his own seed.

One of themselves, even a prophet of their own, said, The Cretians are alway liars, evil beasts, slow bellies [Titus 1:12].

"Evil beasts" means the Cretans were rude and cruel. "Slow bellies" means lazy gluttons. Paul is not being very complimentary here, is he? But this is the reputation they had in the Roman world of Paul's day. Paul is quoting a Cretan poet, Epimenides, who was born in Crete several centuries earlier. Another poet wrote, "Crete, which a hundred cities doth maintain, cannot deny this, though to lying given." Paul said, "Cretians are alway liars." This does not mean that everybody who lived in Crete was a liar anymore than when you say that all

Scottish people are tightfisted—some are very generous. But the Cretans had the general reputation of being liars.

It is marvelous what the grace of God can do and did do among the people of Crete. They were liars, beastly, lazy people, who were big eaters. Many of them turned to Christ, and their lives were changed.

This witness is true. Wherefore rebuke them sharply, that they may be sound in the faith [Titus 1:13].

Paul tells Titus that he is going to have to be a little more strict with the Cretans than he would with others because of their background and their very nature.

Not giving heed to Jewish fables, and commandments of men, that turn from the truth [Titus 1:14].

"Not giving heed to Jewish fables." Paul's reference here is not just to legalism. There grew up around the Mosaic Law a great deal of writing which includes the Talmud and much more. I have not read very much in these Jewish writings because they never really interested me. But I have read some, and there are some pretty wild tales in them.

"Commandments of men, that turn from the truth." The Lord Jesus rebuked the religious rulers for adding traditions to God's law, and that is what Paul is talking about here. The teaching of legalism is in two phases—one is that you are *saved* by the Law, and the other is that you are to *live* by the Law. Both of these teachings are very dangerous. We are saved by the grace of God and are actually called to live on a higher plane than that of the Ten Commandments. God gave the Ten Commandments to a *nation*, and I feel that they should be the law of the world today. When God says, "Thou shalt not kill," that is for everyone, Christian and non-Christian—that is for the whole world. However, those who are saved by the grace of God are given instructions for living which are on an even higher plane than that.

Unto the pure all things are pure: but unto them that are defiled and unbelieving is nothing pure; but even their mind and conscience is defiled [Titus 1:15].

This is the verse that is used by the folk who say that if we are saved by grace it doesn't make any difference how we live; that is, if we are saved, we are pure and can live in any way we like. Certain cults have developed this teaching, saying they can live in sin (they don't call it sin—it's not sin for them) because "unto the pure all things are pure."

What Paul is talking about has nothing to do with *moral* issues at all. He is speaking to this issue of legalism and the eating of meats. The teaching of many legalistic cults often includes a very unusual diet. But Paul says, "Unto the pure all things are pure." In other words, whether you eat meat or don't eat meat makes no difference at all. All food is clean. If you want to eat rattlesnake meat, that is your business; it's my business to keep away from it if I can! You can eat anything you want—"unto the pure all things are pure."

If you are an unbeliever, any special diet you might concoct will make no difference in your relationship to God—it will not save you. You can eat all the vegetables you want, but if you are not right with God, they will not make you pure. The Lord Jesus said that it is not the thing that goes into a man that defiles him, but what comes out of him (see Matt. 15:18–20).

They profess that they know God; but in works they deny him, being abominable, and disobedient, and unto every good work reprobate [Titus 1:16].

"They profess that they know God; but in works they deny him." Many believers today can deny and do deny God by the lives that they live. And they deny the Word of God. I knew a man who was an officer in the church, and he carried the biggest Bible I have ever seen. When he put it under his arm, he leaned to that side! Everybody believed him to be very pious, but outside the church he had the reputation of not really being honest. He carried a big Bible, but he didn't really believe it. You see, you can deny the Bible by the life you live, and you can deny God by the life you live.

"Being abominable, and disobedient, and unto every good work reprobate." Ceremonies and rituals cannot change the evil heart of man. Only the Word of God can change the human heart. When the heart is changed, the life will reveal the change. Paul and James were never in disagreement—they both said that faith without works is dead. Saving faith produces a godly life. As Calvin said, "Faith alone saves, but the faith that saves is not alone."

CHAPTER 2

THEME: The church is to teach and preach the Word of God

THE CHURCH MUST TEACH SOUND DOCTRINE

The church must teach sound doctrine or it is not a church. I have written a little book entitled *The Spiritual Fingerprints of the Visible Church* in which I go back to the Day of Pentecost where we are told that those who were added to the church on that day ". . . continued stedfastly in the apostles' doctrine and fellowship, and in breaking of bread, and in prayers" (Acts 2:42). These were the identification marks of the early church: the apostles' doctrine, fellowship, breaking of bread, and prayer. It really doesn't matter how high the steeple may be or how beautifully the chimes may play, it is the message that is going out from the pulpit which will tell you whether the church is really a church, organized as Paul understood it and as the Word of God declares it.

In the first chapter we found that the elders whom Titus was to ordain were to be able to do two things: to exhort and to refute or confute the heretics. It is important not to spend your entire ministry refuting everybody. There are some men who have what I would call a negative ministry—all they do is attack the enemies of the gospel. That is important, but I believe we all need a balanced ministry. An elder should be able to exhort from the Word of God as well as be able to answer a heretic. In this second chapter Paul's emphasis will be upon the teaching of the Word of God.

But speak thou the things which become sound doctrine [Titus 2:1].

"Sound doctrine" means the apostles' doctrine. The number one thing of importance to the early church was the apostles' doctrine. What we read in these epistles is also a part of the apostles' doctrine, by the way.

First of all, Paul has a message for the senior citizen—for the senior citizen who is male and for the senior citizen who is female.

That the aged men be sober, grave, temperate, sound in faith, in charity, in patience [Titus 2:2].

They are to be sound in their love and in patience. They are to be "sober," that is, very vigilant, very serious. They should be men who are respected and self-controlled.

The aged women likewise, that they be in behaviour as becometh holiness, not false accusers, not given to much wine, teachers of good things [Titus 2:3].

"In behavior as becometh holiness"—the aged women are to be reverent in their behavior.

"Not false accusers," that is, not gossips, and "not given to much wine," or not drunkards. "Teachers of good things." The older women are to teach the younger women:

That they may teach the young women to be sober, to love their husbands, to love their children,

To be discreet, chaste, keepers at home, good, obedient to their own husbands, that the word of God be not blasphemed [Titus 2:4–5].

"Keepers at home" means they are to be workers at home. I may get in trouble here, but I must say this: A wife's first responsibility is in her home. The home is not a playpen; it is a serious responsibility to be a wife and to care for children in the home. It is not something to be taken lightly.

I am confident that Paul would never have approved of the women's lib movement. I will stick my neck out even further and say that I am opposed to it—I think it's wrong. I believe that a woman wants to be treated like a woman and not like a man. I was in a large business establishment recently where there were fifty stenographers, and from what I heard they were really promoting women's lib in that office. I agree that women should be promoted according to their ability and paid according to their ability, but I noticed when we came to get on the elevator the ladies felt like they should get on first. I let them do that because I was taught to do so. If these women really want equality in every way, they should not be working just in offices, but they should also take work as ditchdiggers. However, I am convinced that that is not really what they want. My friend, the biggest and most important business in the world is the making of a home.

"Good" means kindly.

"Obedient to their own husbands." The idea of obedience here is that the women should *respond* to their husbands. Paul uses the same Greek word in Romans 8:7 where it is translated "subject." He says there, "Because the carnal mind is enmity against God: for it is not *subject* to the law of God, neither indeed can be" (italics mine). Paul's thought is that the natural man *cannot* respond to God; he cannot obey God; he has no way to respond to God. Now the wife is to respond to her husband; he is the aggressor, and she is to respond to him.

A great, big, brawny fellow once came to see me in my office, and he said, "I want you to talk to my wife and tell her to obey me!" I told him I would do nothing of the kind, and he asked me why. I said, "When's the last time you told your wife that you loved her?" He couldn't remember and said, "What has that got to do with it?" I told him, "That has everything in the world to do with it! Until you tell her that you love her, I don't see why she should respond to you. Didn't you tell her you loved her when you were courting? Well, just keep that up. The thing to do is to just keep up the courtship. You keep telling her that you love her, and she will respond to you a great deal better than she has been." The wife is to respond to the love of her husband.

Young men likewise exhort to be sober minded [Titus 2:6].

Now Paul turns his attention to the young men, and he probably means that Titus is the one who is to teach the young men.

> **In all things shewing thyself a pattern of good works: in doctrine shewing uncorruptness, gravity, sincerity [Titus 2:7].**

Paul says to this young preacher Titus, "You be a pattern, an example, for the other young men."

"In doctrine shewing uncorruptness." "Uncorruptness" has the idea of incorruptness—that is, in his teaching he is to show his complete faith in the Word of God and appreciate the seriousness of the matters with which he is dealing.

> **Sound speech, that cannot be condemned; that he that is of the contrary part may be ashamed, having no evil thing to say of you [Titus 2:8].**

In other words, your conversation should reveal the fact that you are a child of God.

> **Exhort servants to be obedient unto their own masters, and to please them well in all things; not answering again [Titus 2:9].**

"Exhort servants"—now Paul turns his attention to another group. In the early church there were many slaves. In fact, 90 percent of the names on the walls of the catacombs are those of slaves or ex-slaves. The gospel met a great need for this class of people in that day.

"To be obedient unto their own masters, and to please them well in all things." Again, the idea behind obedience is that they should respond to their masters, be interested in them and in their work. Anyone, especially those in Christian work, should put their heart into their job or else get out of it. If you work for a Christian organization, you do it because you *want* to work for it. I hope you get a good living out of it, but that is not the point. Christian work is to be done with the heart as well as with the head and hands.

"Not answering again," that is, not talking back to your employer.

Not purloining, but shewing all good fidelity; that they may adorn the doctrine of God our Saviour in all things [Titus 2:10].

"Not purloining" means not stealing. Businesses lose many millions of dollars each year because employees steal from them. "Not purloining" means you should not be a thief.

"But shewing all good fidelity"—showing faithfulness.

"That they may adorn the doctrine of God our Saviour in all things." The Greek word for "adorn" is the same word from which we got our English word *cosmetics*. I am often asked whether I feel Christian women should wear makeup. I would say yes, the kind Paul is speaking of here, and plenty of it. "Adorn the doctrine of God"—in other words, if you are sound in the faith, you should be wearing the appropriate cosmetics. I would like to see more of the lipstick of a kind tongue. Speaking kindly is a mighty fine lipstick. And then the face powder of sincerity and reality. My, there are all kinds of cosmetics that you should use today as a Christian.

THE CHURCH MUST PREACH THE GRACE OF GOD

Now Paul interrupts these admonitions to put a doctrinal foundation under the lives of these people. He states the gospel, and he states it in three time zones—the past, the present, and the future.

I grew up in the horse-and-buggy days, and I never cease to wonder at the speed of jet travel. Beside the actual speed of the planes, the crossing of time zones makes it possible to arrive at the end of a three- or four-hour flight and see that it is only an hour later than it was when you started. I understand they are working now on a plane that will travel three times the speed of sound. That means you could leave Dallas, Texas, and arrive in Los Angeles two hours before you left Dallas! That would be a wonderful thing.

However, I think the most wonderful thing in the world is that the grace of God is in three time zones. We see that in the next three verses: "For the grace of God that bringeth salvation hath appeared"

(v. 11)—that's the past time zone; "teaching us" (v. 12)—that's the present time zone of grace; and "looking for that blessed hope" (v. 13)—that is the future time zone. These, then, are the three time zones of grace. Let us look at them a little more closely:

For the grace of God that bringeth salvation hath appeared to all men [Titus 2:11].

Paul says to the Cretans, "I want to put under you the doctrine of the grace of God because you need a solid foundation." The grace of God is the way God saves us. Years ago I heard a great preacher, Dr. Dodd, in Shreveport, Louisiana, say, "My pulpit is a place for good news; my study is the place for good advice." The gospel is not good advice—it is good *news*. It is even more than that; it is the power of God unto salvation.

Paul is enjoining Titus to demand of the Cretans that they live lives that adorn the gospel, for it is the *power* of God. There is absolutely no excuse for any Christian to live a life of defeat and failure—"for the grace of God that bringeth salvation hath appeared to all men."

"Hath appeared" means it shines forth—it is the epiphany. What the Lord Jesus did for us when He came more than nineteen hundred years ago is the gospel, the good news. He died for us, and He rose again. God doesn't save us by His love, and He doesn't save us by His mercy. Ephesians tells us: "For by *grace* are ye saved through faith; and that not of yourselves: it is the gift of God" (Eph. 2:8, italics mine). *Mercy* is the compassion of God that prompted Him to send a Savior to mankind. If one man could be saved by the mercy of God, all mankind would be saved. It wouldn't have been necessary for Christ to die; the Cross would have been circumvented. God loves men, but He didn't save us by His love. *Love* is the divine motive, but God is not only love, He is righteous and holy and just. The holy demands of God, His just claims, and His righteous standard had to be met. The love of God may long to save us, but the immutable law of justice makes love powerless to do so. Therefore, Christ, by dying for our sins, met the holy demands of God's justice, and He can now save us by *grace*. How wonderful it is to be saved by the grace of God! When we were guilty, Christ paid the penalty. Grace is not complicated or implicated with human effort. God doesn't ask your cooperation; He doesn't ask for your conduct or your character in order to save you. God only asks men to believe Him, to trust Him, and to accept Christ. God's way is the best way, and it is the *only* way.

> **Teaching us that, denying ungodliness and worldly lusts, we should live soberly, righteously, and godly, in this present world [Titus 2:12].**

God is not trying to reform this world; He is redeeming men who accept Christ. The gospel does not appeal to Christ-rejecting men to do better. When a person says, "I am going to try to do better," I think he is a liar. If you have rejected Jesus Christ, you might as well try to get all you can out of this life, because this life is all that you are going to get. Today our government is trying to get people to stop smoking; they're trying to educate people to the dangers of cigarettes. However, God is not asking you to do such things. You might as well eat, drink, and be merry, for tomorrow you'll die. God doesn't want to reform you; He wants to redeem you.

"Teaching us"—*teaching* means child-training. God *is* calling those who are His own, who are redeemed, to live for Him and to avoid "worldly lusts."

> **Looking for that blessed hope, and the glorious appearing of the great God and our Saviour Jesus Christ [Titus 2:13].**

"Looking for that blessed hope"—this is the next happening in the program of God: Christ is coming to take His church out of this world.

"The glorious appearing of the great God and our Saviour Jesus Christ." This reveals that Paul taught the deity of Christ; he speaks of the great God who is our Savior, and who is He? He is Jesus Christ. And what did He do?—

Who gave himself for us, that he might redeem us from all iniquity, and purify unto himself a peculiar people, zealous of good works [Titus 2:14].

He gave Himself for us that He might redeem us. He paid a price for us that He might redeem us "from all iniquity."

"And purify unto himself a peculiar people, zealous of good works." "A peculiar people" would be better translated "a people for His possession." It is true that God wants you to live for Him and wants you to do good works, but He will have to redeem you first, my friend.

These things speak, and exhort, and rebuke with all authority. Let no man despise thee [Titus 2:15].

Paul says to Titus, "You are a young man. Don't let them despise you because of the life you live." Titus should be able to teach all these things with authority.

This has been a wonderful epistle. Every young preacher ought to study carefully the Book of Titus.

CHAPTER 3

THEME: The church is to perform good works

This epistle gives us the picture which covers the entire spectrum of what God wants for the church. We saw in the first chapter that God wants the church to be an orderly organization. Then we saw in the next chapter that the church is to be sound in doctrine. Now we shall learn that, to be all that God wants for the church, the church is to perform good works.

GOOD WORKS ARE AN EVIDENCE OF SALVATION

Put them in mind to be subject to principalities and powers, to obey magistrates, to be ready to every good work [Titus 3:1].

The very first thing he mentions here is the fact that the church must have members who are law abiding. A believer should obey the laws of the land in which he lives unless those laws conflict or contradict his duty and relationship to God.

I always felt embarrassed when I taught evening Bible classes in downtown Los Angeles and would be requested to announce that someone had parked in a *no parking* place. Or sometimes I had to announce that a car was blocking a driveway so that the people who owned the driveway couldn't get out. That kind of parking was breaking the law on the part of someone in my class who apparently didn't pay very much attention to the fact that a Christian is to be subject to principalities and powers.

Now that brings up the question of what a believer should do when the laws of the land conflict with his duty and relationship to God. For example, should a young man who is drafted into military service go out to war when his real Christian conviction tells him otherwise? Fortunately in our country such a young man with real convictions against war can be a conscientious objector. He need not go into the

armed forces to carry a gun, but he can spend the same amount of time
as the other young men in the army but be assigned noncombat duties. I think any young man should be commended for that, because I
believe it takes courage and conviction for a young man under those
circumstances to stand on his two feet and say, "Yes, I'll serve; I'll
wear the uniform, but I cannot conscientiously carry a gun." I think
that sympathy and understanding should be granted to such a young
man.

On the other hand, there have been many young men in this country who have run away to escape the draft. They did not run away
because of religious conviction. I can't think of any other explanation
than that they were disloyal to their country. They were not obedient
to this nation. These young men wanted to enjoy all the blessings and
bebefits of our nation but did not want to meet its responsibilities.
They have broken the law and should pay the penalty.

We are to be subject to the principalities and powers over us. A
church should teach this; part of the message that should be given to
church members is that they should be obedient to the powers that be.
That obedience is not to the *man* but to the *office* that he represents.
Perhaps you resent the manner in which a police officer gives you a
citation for a traffic violation, but you should respect the uniform he
wears. He represents the segment of our society that protects our persons and our property. Without them we would be in a bad way today.

This verse also raises the question of whether a Christian should
go into politics or not. I believe that the individual Christian is free to
go into politics, but I do not believe that the church should go into
politics. If we would have a real moving of the Spirit of God, many of
the men from our churches would go into these different offices in
government today.

A good example of this is the Wesleyan movement in England.
Wesley never tried to straighten out the king of England or even the
Church of England. He just went out and preached the Word of God.
Men were converted, among whom were men like William Wilber-
force, the great philanthropist and abolitionist. They were men who
had been gamblers and drunkards, with no concern for the poor, until
they came to know Christ. These men started the great labor move-

ment associated with the Wesleyan revival in England, which was the beginning of the movement against child labor and the protection of workmen on the job. We need individuals who will enter into government and take social action, but the church as an organization is not called upon to go into politics.

"To be ready to every good work." The church is to instruct individuals to be eager, to be anxious, and to learn to perform good works. We'll note this as we go along.

Now there is also a negative side to the exhortation:

To speak evil of no man, to be no brawlers, but gentle, shewing all meekness unto all men [Titus 3:2].

"Speak evil of no man" means we are to malign no one, and we are not to repeat gossip. It has been said that you can't *believe* everything you hear today, but you can *repeat* it! That is what he is talking about here—we are *not* to repeat what we hear. Many evil reports are passed from person to person without even a shred of evidence that the report is true. Another old saying is that some people will believe anything if it is *whispered* to them!

However, if the church has solid evidence that a member is doing something evil, that member should be named. You may remember that Paul named certain men who were evil men: Phygellus and Hermogenes, Hymenaeus and Philetus, and Alexander the coppersmith. Then he also said that Demas had forsaken him, having loved this present world.

For we ourselves also were sometimes foolish, disobedient, deceived, serving divers lusts and pleasures, living in malice and envy, hateful, and hating one another [Titus 3:3].

This is a picture of the unsaved today, and a picture of you and me before we knew Christ. We were foolish, disobedient, deceived, enslaved to lusts and pleasures, living selfishly, and hating others. That is a picture of the lost world.

You can go to visit in non-Christian homes, and you will find these things. Go into any business, any office, any factory, and you will see these things present. Unfortunately, you can see some of these same things in our churches. There can be a pretense of loving, but under it there is envying and hating and gossiping. You can find churches divided into little cliques and groups; yet they boast about how sound they are in the faith. That is a disgrace to the cause of Christ. This is a picture of the unsaved given to us here. It ought never to be a picture of you or me as believers.

> **But after that the kindness and love of God our Saviour toward man appeared,**
>
> **Not by works of righteousness which we have done, but according to his mercy he saved us, by the washing of regeneration, and renewing of the Holy Ghost [Titus 3:4–5].**

"Not by works of righteousness which we have done." Verse 3 gave us a picture of how we were before we came to know Christ. It is important to understand that becoming a Christian doesn't mean just turning over a new leaf—you will find yourself writing on the new leaf the same things that you wrote on the old leaf. Making New Year's resolutions and promising to do better doesn't make you a Christian. Nor are you saved on the basis of works of righteousness, good deeds, which you have done.

"But according to his mercy he saved us." Because Christ died for us and paid the penalty for our sins, God is prepared to extend mercy to us; it is according to His mercy that He saved us. And He is rich in mercy, which means He has plenty of it. Whoever you are, He can save you today because Christ died for you. He paid the penalty and makes over to you His righteousness!

"By the washing of regeneration." "Washing" means *laver*—it is the laver of regeneration. In the Old Testament the laver, which stood in the court of the tabernacle and later the temple, represented this.

This washing of regeneration is what the Lord was speaking about in the third chapter of John: ". . . Except a man be born of water and of the Spirit, he cannot enter into the kingdom of God" (John 3:5). The water represents the Word of God—the Bible will *wash* you. It has a sanctifying power, a cleansing power. We are cleansed by the Word of God. The Holy Spirit uses the Word of God—"born of water and of the Spirit." That is the way we are born again.

"And renewing of the Holy Ghost"—He regenerates us.

Which he shed on us abundantly through Jesus Christ our Saviour [Titus 3:6].

Have you noticed that in everything God does there is a surplus? He is able to do exceeding abundantly above all that we ask or think.

That being justified by his grace, we should be made heirs according to the hope of eternal life [Titus 3:7].

"The hope of eternal life" is again pointing to the great hope of the believer, the coming of Christ for His church.

GOOD WORKS ARE PROFITABLE FOR THE PRESENT AND FUTURE

This is a faithful saying, and these things I will that thou affirm constantly, that they which have believed in God might be careful to maintain good works. These things are good and profitable unto men [Titus 3:8].

The fact that the believer is saved by the grace of God does not excuse him from performing good works. The fact of the matter is, he is to "be careful to maintain good works." Paul says that Titus should just keep affirming this constantly.

My friend, after you have been saved, God is going to talk to you about good works. Until that time, God is not even interested in your "good works" because what you call a good work, God calls dirty laundry. The righteousness of man is filthy rags in His sight (see Isa.

64:6). He doesn't want any of that. He wants to *save* you. If you do come to Him just as you are, He will save you, because He has *done* something for you. He is not asking you to do something—what could you do for God? After you are saved, after you are a child of God, then He wants to talk to you about producing good works. He wants you to get involved in getting out the Word of God to others.

"Be *careful* to maintain good works." These are things that you should think about and consider; ponder, be anxious to be producing works for God.

> **But avoid foolish questions, and genealogies, and contentions, and strivings about the law; for they are unprofitable and vain [Titus 3:9].**

We are to defend the faith, Paul says, but we are not to do it by argument or debate. That does no good; that never led anyone to the Lord. You may whip a man down intellectually by your arguments, but that does not touch his heart and win him for Christ. Stay away from foolish questions and genealogies and contentions.

That is the reason I do not develop certain subjects that are sensational. For example, during this period of time in which I am writing, demonism seems to be the topic of the hour. I have had any number of letters saying, "Dr. McGee, give a series on demonism. Write a book about it." Let's not get involved in that kind of thing. I would much rather tell you about the Holy Spirit who can indwell you. If He is in you, no demon could ever possess you! ". . . greater is he that is in you, than he that is in the world" (1 John 4:4). That is what we need to know. It is so easy to get sidetracked.

> **A man that is an heretic after the first and second admonition reject [Titus 3:10].**

We have been asked to join in certain projects in which there are some heretics. I am not interested in being joined with anyone who has views that are in opposition to the Word of God. God tells us here to be separate from heretics. Just let them alone; reject them.

> **Knowing that he that is such is subverted, and sinneth,
> being condemned of himself [Titus 3:11].**

The heretic is one who has turned aside from the truth.

> **When I shall send Artemas unto thee, or Tychicus, be
> diligent to come unto me to Nicopolis: for I have deter-
> mined there to winter.**
>
> **Bring Zenas the lawyer and Apollos on their journey
> diligently, that nothing be wanting unto them.**
>
> **And let ours also learn to maintain good works for nec-
> essary uses, that they be not unfruitful [Titus 3:12–14].**

Paul gives a final admonition about good works. We must "learn" to
maintain good works. It's something that must be worked at. A great
many people think it is easy; we need to know what God considers
good works, and we need to *learn* how to do them.

Paul concludes this practical letter to Titus with a benediction.

> **All that are with me salute thee. Greet them that love us
> in the faith. Grace be with you all. Amen [Titus 3:15].**

(For Bibliography to Titus, see Bibliography at the end of 2 Timothy.)

PHILEMON

The Epistle to
PHILEMON

INTRODUCTION

This is one of the most remarkable epistles in the Scripture. It is only one chapter; so you may have trouble finding it. If you can find Titus, just keep on going; if you find Hebrews, you have gone too far.

The Epistles (letters) in the New Testament were a new form of revelation. Before them, God had used law, history, poetry, prophecy, and the gospel records. When God used the Epistles, He adopted a more personal and direct method. And there are different kinds of epistles. Some were directed to churches; some were directed to individuals and are rather intimate.

Frankly, I believe that Paul had no idea his letter to Philemon would be included in the canon of Scripture, and I think he would be a little embarrassed. Reading this epistle is like looking over the shoulder of Philemon and reading his personal mail. Paul wrote this letter to him personally. That does not detract from the inspiration and value of this epistle. The Holy Spirit has included it in the Scriptures for a very definite reason.

Behind this epistle there is a story, of course. Philemon lived in a place called Colossae. It was way up in the Phrygian country in the Anatolian section of what is Turkey today. No city is there today—just ruins. But it was a great city in Paul's day. One of Paul's epistles was written to the Colossian believers. There is no record that Paul ever visited Colossae, but since there are many things we do not know, I suspect that Paul did visit that city.

The story of this epistle was enacted on the black background of slavery. There were approximately sixty million slaves in the Roman Empire where the total population did not exceed one hundred twenty million. A slave was a chattel. He was treated worse than an enemy. He was subject to the whim of his master.

In Colossae was this very rich man who had come to a saving faith in Christ. He apparently had come down to Ephesus, as Paul was there for two years speaking in the school of Tyrannus every day, and people were coming in from all over that area to hear him. There were millions of people in Asia Minor, and Philemon was just one of the men who came to know the Lord Jesus.

Now Philemon owned slaves, and he had a slave named Onesimus. Onesimus took a chance one day, as any slave would have done, and made a run for it. He did what most runaway slaves apparently did—he moved into a great metropolis. This slave made it all the way to Rome. In that great population, he could be buried, as it were, and never be recognized.

One day, this man Onesimus, who had been a slave, found out that there was a slavery in freedom and there was a freedom in slavery. When he was a slave, he didn't worry about where he was going to sleep or what he was going to eat. His master had to take care of that. Now he has a real problem in Rome. I can imagine him going down the street one day and seeing a group of people gathered around listening to a man. Onesimus wormed his way into the crowd, got up front, and saw that the man was in chains. Onesimus had run away from chains, and he thought he was free, but when he listened to that man—by the way, his name was Paul—he thought, *That man's free, and I'm still a slave—a slave to appetite, a slave to the economy. I'm still a slave, but that man, although he is chained, is free.*

Onesimus waited until the others had drifted away and then went up to Paul. He wanted to know more about what Paul was preaching, and Paul led him to Christ; that is, he presented the gospel to him, told him how Jesus had died for him and how He had been buried but rose again on the third day. He asked Onesimus to put his trust in Christ, and he did. Onesimus became a new creation in Christ Jesus.

Then Onesimus did what any man does who has been converted; he thought back on his past life and the things which were wrong that he wanted to make right. He said to Paul, "Paul, there is something I must confess to you. I'm a runaway slave." Paul asked him where he had come from, and Onesimus told Paul it was from Asia Minor, from the city of Colossae. Paul said, "There's a church over there. Who was your master?"

"My master was Philemon."

"You mean Philemon who lives on Main Street?"

"Yes."

"Why, he is one of my converts also. He owes me a great deal."

"Well, Paul, do you think I should go back to him?"

"Yes, you should. Onesimus, you must go back, but you are going to go back to a different situation. I will send a letter with you."

And we have his letter before us—the Epistle of Paul to Philemon.

In the human heart there has always been a great desire to be free. But right now there are millions of Americans who are slaves to alcohol. They are not free. They are alcoholics. Then there are those who are slaves to drugs. There are those who are slaves to the economy. There are slaves to the almighty dollar. We are living in a day when people pride themselves on being free. They think they are free, but the Lord Jesus said, "If the Son makes you free, then are you free indeed" (see John 8:36). You will not get arguments for or against slavery from this epistle. What you do learn is the freedom that is above all the slavery of this world. It is the freedom that every one of us wants to have.

OUTLINE

PHILEMON

THEME: Revelation of Christ's love for us; demonstration of how brotherly love should work

The primary purpose of this epistle is to reveal Christ's love for us in what He did for us in pleading our case before God. This is one of the finest illustrations of substitution. "If he hath wronged thee, or oweth thee aught, put that on mine account" (v. 18). We can hear Christ agreeing to take our place and to have all our sin imputed to Him. He took our place in death, but He gives us His place in life. "If thou count me therefore a partner, receive him as myself" (v. 17). We have the standing of Christ before God, or we have no standing at all. Onesimus, the unprofitable runaway slave, was to be received as Paul, the great apostle, would have been received in the home of Philemon.

The practical purpose is to teach brotherly love. Paul spoke of the new relationship between master and servant in the other Prison Epistles. Here he demonstrates how it should work. These men, belonging to two different classes in the Roman Empire, hating each other and hurting each other, are now brothers in Christ, and they are to act like it. This is the only solution to the problem of capital and labor.

GENIAL GREETING TO PHILEMON AND HIS FAMILY

Paul, a prisoner of Jesus Christ, and Timothy our brother, unto Philemon our dearly beloved, and fellow-labourer [Philem. 1].

Paul does not mention the fact that he is an apostle. When he was writing to the churches, he gave his official title: an apostle of Jesus Christ. But this is a personal letter to a personal friend. He doesn't need to defend his apostleship. He intended for this to be very personal, and I think he would really be surprised to know it can be read by the whole world.

"Paul, a prisoner of Jesus Christ." I have noticed that several of the commentaries try to change this and explain it away by teaching that Paul really meant that he was a prisoner because he was preaching the gospel of Jesus Christ. But that is not what Paul said, and Paul had the ability of saying exactly what he had in mind. He was using the Greek language, which is a very flexible, versatile language. He said he was a prisoner of Jesus Christ.

If we had been there we might have had a conversation with Paul like this:

"Poor Paul, it's too bad these Romans put you in jail."

"They didn't put me in jail."

"Oh, we know what you mean. Those hateful religious rulers brought a charge against you."

"They didn't put me in jail either."

"Who put you in jail, then?"

"Jesus Christ. I'm *His* prisoner."

"You mean to tell me that you would serve Someone who would put you in prison?"

"Yes, when it's His will for me to be in prison, I'm in prison. When it's His will for me to be out of prison, I'll be out of prison. When it's His will for me to be sick, I'm going to be sick. I belong to Him. Since I belong to Him, I have learned to be content in whatsoever state I am in. Everything is all right. Don't worry about me."

Obviously, the letter to Philemon is one of the Prison Epistles. It goes along with Ephesians, Philippians, and Colossians.

"And Timothy our brother" is really "and Timothy *the* brother." That means he is not only Philemon's brother and Paul's brother, but he is *your* brother if you are a Christian. We all are brothers in Christ.

"Unto Philemon our dearly beloved." Does that sound as if Paul is really buttering him up? I think so. But he loved this man, and he is going to make a request of him.

And to our beloved Apphia, and Archippus our fellow-soldier, and to the church in thy house [Philem. 2].

"And to our beloved Apphia." She apparently was the wife of Philemon. While *Philemon* is a Greek name, and he was a citizen of Colossae, *Apphia* is a Phrygian name. That would suggest to me that a young businessman by the name of Philemon went into new territory. He didn't go west as a young man; he went east—way up on the frontier. He got into business in Colossae and became a wealthy man there. He met and married a Phrygian girl named Apphia. They both now have become Christians. Isn't that lovely?

"And Archippus our fellow-soldier." I would assume this is their son. He is not a soldier of the Roman army, but a soldier in the army of Jesus Christ. Paul had written elsewhere that we all are to be good soldiers of Jesus Christ.

"And to the church in thy house." Not only had they been converted, but they had a church in their house. Let's think about this for a moment. The church building has become so all-important to people today that it is all out of relationship to the real purpose of the local church. The local church in Paul's day wasn't down on the corner in a separate building—they didn't have any building. There were the great temples to the pagan gods, but the early church didn't have buildings; they met in homes. It is estimated that for two hundred years the church met in homes.

The great cathedrals of the past were actually never meant for public meetings. Westminster Abbey in England, for example, was never intended for public services. It was built in the shape of a cross as a monument to Jesus Christ. Although I think they had the wrong idea—instead of spending all that money on a cathedral, they should have used it to send out missionaries—that was their way of expressing their devotion. The idea of putting the emphasis on a building and on a building program is a little out of line with the example of the early church.

Grace to you, and peace, from God our Father and the Lord Jesus Christ [Philem. 3].

This is the usual greeting of Paul to every person and every church to which he wrote.

GOOD REPUTATION OF PHILEMON

I thank my God, making mention of thee always in my prayers [Philem. 4].

Here is a man for whom Paul prayed. If you are writing out a prayer list of the apostle Paul, be sure to put Philemon on that list. The thought here is that every time Philemon's name was mentioned, Paul prayed for him. This would indicate that Philemon was a rather prominent person.

Hearing of thy love and faith, which thou hast toward the Lord Jesus, and toward all saints [Philem. 5].

The life of Philemon was a testimony. Paul describes it in a lovely way. He showed love toward the Lord Jesus and toward other believers. His faith was toward the Lord Jesus, and he was faithful to other believers. That is interesting.

That the communication of thy faith may become effectual by the acknowledging of every good thing which is in you in Christ Jesus [Philem. 6].

His faith was shared. The life of Philemon was a testimony. "Every good thing" was the result of the fact that ". . . it is God which worketh in you both to will and to do of his good pleasure" (Phil. 2:13).

For we have great joy and consolation in thy love, because the bowels of the saints are refreshed by thee, brother [Philem. 7].

Paul had great joy and consolation in the love of Philemon for other believers and for him.

"Bowels" or *heart* implies the entire psychological nature. It is the inner life of the believers that had great satisfaction through him.

There are many wonderful Christians across this land whom I have had the privilege of meeting, of being in their homes, and of having fellowship with them. That has been one of the greatest joys of my ministry. Philemon was the kind of person who would have entertained evangelists and conference speakers in his home. He was a marvelous individual.

GRACIOUS PLEA FOR ONESIMUS

Wherefore, though I might be much bold in Christ to enjoin thee that which is convenient,

Yet for love's sake I rather beseech thee, being such an one as Paul the aged, and now also a prisoner of Jesus Christ [Philem. 8–9].

Paul is making a gracious plea for Onesimus. He is coming to the purpose of his letter. He approaches his subject diplomatically and cautiously and lovingly. He is going to make his request for Onesimus on a threefold basis:

"For love's sake." This is the love of Paul and Philemon for each other as believers in Christ Jesus.

"Being such an one as Paul the aged." Paul was only in his sixties, but he was an old man. He had suffered and had been persecuted as a missionary for Christ. This had aged him. Paul says to Philemon, "You know that I am an old man now."

"A prisoner of Jesus Christ." It is evident that he could not come to Philemon in person.

I beseech thee for my son Onesimus, whom I have begotten in my bonds [Philem. 10].

Paul is pleading on behalf of his son. Paul was not married, but he had many sons. He calls Timothy and Titus his sons, and now Onesimus. These are his spiritual sons. He had led Onesimus to the Lord even though he himself was a prisoner at the time.

Which in time past was to thee unprofitable, but now profitable to thee and to me [Philem. 11].

The name *Onesimus* means "profitable." Paul really has a play on words here that is tremendous. He is good at that, by the way. Since his name literally means profitable, Paul is saying, "When you had Profitable, you didn't have Profitable. Now that you don't have Profitable, you do have Profitable." You see, as a slave Onesimus wasn't very useful. He didn't work because he wanted to work. His heart wasn't in it, and I guess I can't blame him for that. But now Paul is sending him back to Philemon as a believer, and he says, "He is going to be profitable to you now. However, I don't want him to be received as a slave."

> **Whom I have sent again: thou therefore receive him, that is, mine own bowels:**
>
> **Whom I would have retained with me, that in thy stead he might have ministered unto me in the bonds of the gospel [Philem. 12–13].**

Paul is asking Philemon to receive Onesimus just as if he were receiving Paul. Now Paul admits that he would have liked to have kept Onesimus. I'm sure Paul would say, "My first thought was that this man knows how to serve, and I need somebody. I am here in prison, old and sick and cold. This fellow could help me. My first thought was to keep him here and just let you know that I have him here with me." But Paul couldn't do that. He says—

> **But without thy mind would I do nothing; that thy benefit should not be as it were of necessity, but willingly [Philem. 14].**

Paul is saying, "I wouldn't keep Onesimus because that wouldn't be right—although I thought of it. If you willingly want to send him back to me, that will be all right." Did Philemon send Onesimus back to Paul? Again, that is something we do not know. I think he did. I would imagine that on the next boat going to Rome, there was Onesimus with a lot of things to add to Paul's comfort.

For perhaps he therefore departed for a season, that thou shouldest receive him for ever;

Not now as a servant, but above a servant, a brother beloved, specially to me, but how much more unto thee, both in the flesh, and in the Lord? [Philem. 15–16].

Since Onesimus has become a believer, his status and relationship to Philemon are different. He is still a slave according to the Roman law, but he is more than that to Philemon. He is now a beloved brother.

GUILTLESS SUBSTITUTES FOR GUILTY

This verse, together with the next verse, gives us one of the grandest illustrations of full substitution and imputation. Behind Paul's plea is Christ's plea to the Father on behalf of the sinner who trusts Christ as the Savior. That sinner is received on the same standing that Christ is received. In other words, the saved sinner has as much right in heaven as Christ has, for he has His right to be there. We are accepted in the beloved (see Eph. 1:6).

If thou count me therefore a partner, receive him as myself [Philem. 17].

"Since you count me as a partner, I want you to receive him just like you would receive me. You always put me up in that guest room. Don't send him out in the cold; put him up in the guest room."

GLORIOUS ILLUSTRATION OF IMPUTATION

If he hath wronged thee, or oweth thee aught, put that on mine account [Philem. 18].

We think that the credit card is something new in our day. We can buy almost anything with a credit card—from a gallon of gas to a chain of motels. Credit cards are used so much that one restaurant posted the sign: "We take money too."

Paul also had a credit card. He had a credit card because he was a believer in Christ. Paul says, "Look, if Onesimus stole something from you or did something wrong, just put it on my account. Put it on my credit card."

All of this is a glorious picture. When I come to God the Father for salvation, I can hear the Lord Jesus Christ say, "If Vernon McGee has wronged Thee or oweth Thee anything, put that on My account." Christ on the Cross paid the penalty for my sins. But that isn't all. I am sure that God the Father would say, "That fellow Vernon McGee is not fit for heaven." Then the Lord Jesus would say, "If Thou count Me therefore a partner, receive Vernon McGee as Myself." That is what it means to be in Christ—accepted in the Beloved. Oh, what a picture this is of the way God the Father and the Lord Jesus Christ accept you and accept me. That makes this a very precious epistle.

GENERAL AND PERSONAL ITEMS AND REQUESTS

I Paul have written it with mine own hand, I will repay it: albeit I do not say to thee how thou owest unto me even thine own self besides [Philem. 19].

"I Paul have written it with mine own hand, I will repay it." The Lord Jesus Christ gave His life and shed His blood to pay our entire debt of sin.

"Albeit I do not say to thee how thou owest unto me even thine own self besides." Paul had led Philemon to the Lord. How could he ever repay Paul for that?

Yea, brother, let me have joy of thee in the Lord: refresh my bowels in the Lord [Philem. 20].

Paul is pleading for Onesimus.

Having confidence in thy obedience I wrote unto thee, knowing that thou wilt also do more than I say [Philem. 21].

As you can see, this is a personal letter, and in a sense we are reading it over the shoulder of Philemon. Paul expresses his confidence in him and actually feels that Philemon will do more than he requests.

It is characteristic of real believers to do more than is requested. Jesus asks us to go the second mile. Maybe the reason that some of us are so poor today is that we have been stingy with the Lord. The Lord is a generous Lord. We should be generous people.

But withal prepare me also a lodging: for I trust that through your prayers I shall be given unto you [Philem. 22].

Paul expects to be released from prison. He requests prayers for that purpose. Since this letter was probably written during Paul's first confinement in Rome, he was released and probably visited Philemon personally.

There salute thee Epaphras, my fellow-prisoner in Christ Jesus;

Marcus, Aristarchus, Demas, Lucas, my fellow-labourers.

The grace of our Lord Jesus Christ be with your spirit. Amen [Philem. 23–25].

This beautiful little letter concludes with personal greetings to mutual friends.

(For Bibliography to Philemon, see Bibliography at the end of 2 Timothy.)